The Winter that Won the War

THE WINTER ENCAMPMENT AT VALLEY FORGE
1777-1778

by Phillip S. Greenwalt

EMERGING REVOLUTIONARY WAR SERIES

Phillip S. Greenwalt, series editor
Robert Orrison, chief historian

The Emerging Revolutionary War Series

offers compelling, easy-to-read overviews of some of the Revolutionary War's most important battles and stories.

Other titles in the Emerging Revolutionary War Series:

A Single Blow: The Battles of Lexington and Concord and the Beginning of the American Revolution, April 19, 1775
by Phillip S. Greenwalt and Robert Orrison

Victory or Death: The Battles of Trenton and Princeton, December 25, 1776–January 3, 1777
by Mark Maloy

A Handsome Flogging: The Battle of Monmouth Court House, June 28, 1778
by William R. Griffith IV

The Winter that Won the War

THE WINTER ENCAMPMENT AT VALLEY FORGE
1777-1778

by Phillip S. Greenwalt

EMERGING REVOLUTIONARY WAR SERIES

SB

Savas Beatie
California

First edition, first printing

ISBN-13 (paperback): 978-1-61121-493-2
ISBN-13 (ebook): 978-1-61121-494-9

Library of Congress Cataloging-in-Publication Data

Names: Greenwalt, Phillip S., author.
Title: The winter that won the war : the winter encampment at Valley Forge, 1777-1778 / by Phillip S. Greenwalt.
Description: First edition. | El Dorado Hills, California : Savas Beatie, [2021] | Series: Emerging revolutionary war series
Identifiers: LCCN 2019014672| ISBN 9781611214932 (pbk : alk. paper) | ISBN 9781611214949 (ebk)
Subjects: LCSH: United States--History--Revolution, 1775-1783--Campaigns. | Washington, George, 1732-1799--Headquarters--Pennsylvania--Valley Forge. | Valley Forge (Pa.)--History--18th century.
Classification: LCC E234 .G77 2019 | DDC 973.3/32--dc23
LC record available at https://lccn.loc.gov/2019014672

Published by
Savas Beatie LLC

989 Governor Drive, Suite 102
El Dorado Hills, California 95762
Phone: 916-941-6896
Email: sales@savasbeatie.com
Web: www.savasbeatie.com

Savas Beatie titles are available at special discounts for bulk purchases in the United States by corporations, institutions, and other organizations. For more details, please contact Special Sales, 989 Governor Drive, Suite 102, El Dorado Hills, CA 95762, or you may e-mail us at sales@savasbeatie.com, or visit our website at www.savasbeatie.com for additional information.

To all the patriots of Valley Forge...

Table of Contents

List of Maps

Maps by Edward Alexander
Make Me a Map, LLC

Baron von Stueben's appearance, and the discipline and drill he brought with him, was a turning point of the war. (cm)

Acknowledgments

One name may appear on the cover of this book, but many people deserve credit for making this publication a reality. Inspiration and my introduction to history was a direct result of my parents, Stephen and Melanie Greenwalt. From an early age they nurtured my inquisitive nature in history, fueled my interest to learn more about the people of yesteryear, and encouraged me in my career choices. Although my father is battling dementia, the times we spent tramping around battlefields and historic sites are memories I'll cherish forever. A mental illness cannot take that away from him, me, or our family. To my brother, Patrick, and sister, Adrienne: thank you for the encouraging words, trekking the various fields with your older brother, and providing a sounding board for ideas.

(psg)

Gordon Morgan, thank you for reading, re-reading, answering emails, and being a great proofreader and positive influence on the book. Rob Orrison, the co-founder of the series, thank you for doing the same in regard to the history and also making sure I could have a few moments of hilarity as a break from the seriousness of writing this book. Looking forward to reversing roles for your upcoming publication! To Tara Hatmaker for her amazing ability to fit all the various pieces together in layout to make this book come alive, thank you for all your work on this project. Also, to Dan Davis for his insight on Valley Forge during the American Battlefield Trust Teacher Institute in 2018 and also for reviewing one of the appendices for this book. To Chris Mackowski who saw this through to the finish line, thanks for the helping hand.

To Castle, Patty, and Ivan, who strolled around Philadelphia in June 2018, on one of the hottest days of the year to find sites attributed to the 1777-78 campaign. Little did they know when they asked for me to pick them up from a concert and drive them to the airport, there would be a historical detour enroute. Thanks for sweltering in the heat and being a good sport about it all!

To historian Eric Olsen of Morristown National Historical Park, who read over the initial chapters, thank you for lending a critical eye to making this work better. Your wit and sense of humor, along with the discussions of the various encampments, helped bring this history into better focus. To Jonathan Parker, the Chief of Interpretation at Valley Forge National Historical Park, thank you for the positive words, connections, and having staff lend their expertise to the chapters dedicated to the encampment. A thank you needs to be extended as well to Alyse Van De Putte, from the Museum of the American Revolution, for her assistance in gaining access to the Trego painting.

From Ted Savas, to Sarah Keeney, to Mary Gutzke, and the entire Savas Beatie team, thank you for believing in this series and allowing the great crew at Emerging Revolutionary War to share their passion for telling America's military history in book form. Edward Alexander's maps are an invaluable addition to making the hallowed ground accessible to readers. Evan Sharko, a great young historian, journeyed around Pennsylvania and New Jersey to take photographs for me. Thank you! Travis Shaw, another great historian, shared his knowledge on the winter encampment at Wilmington, Delaware, which details another side of the winter that won the war. Mark Maloy reminded us, through a different appendix in this book, about where Valley Forge resides in our collective memory.

For one other person: to "Red," who understands that sharing my passion for American history is the musical cadence my heart beats to.

PHOTO CREDITS:
Phillip S. Greenwalt (psg); Library of Congress (loc); Chris Mackowski (cm); Museum of the American Revolution (moar); National Archives (NA); New York Public Library (nypl); Pennsylvania State Archives (pasa); Terry Rensel (tr); Evan Sharko (es); Wikipedia Commons(wc); Yale (y).

For the Emerging Revolutionary War Series

Theodore P. Savas, *publisher*
Sarah Keeney, *editorial consultant*
Chris Mackowski, *advisory editor*
Phillip S. Greenwalt, *series editor*
Robert Orrison, *chief historian*

Gordon Morgan, *copyeditor*
Maps by Edward Alexander
Design and layout by Tara Hatmaker
and Chris Mackowski

Introduction

Cold. Weary. Tired. Hungry. Poor. Desperate. A painting can evoke a thousand words and almost as many images. William B. T. Trego, a painter best known for his military depictions, put paintbrush to canvas in 1883 to capture one of the most iconic scenes, from his mind, of the American Revolutionary War.

Marching toward Valley Forge, the remnants of the Continental army pass under the steely gaze of Gen. George Washington and his retinue of aides-de-camp and staff officers. Peering closer at the men in column, one sees a miscellaneous collection of clothing loosely suggestive of a uniform. Some soldiers wear tricorn hats, others have shreds of clothing wrapped around their ears to keep warm, while bloody bandages dress wounds received on still others. In the front row a drummer has bare legs, his stockings worn out many steps ago. A few of his comrades display various stages of nakedness. And although not clearly painted, there is evidence that some of the men are tromping through the snow barefooted.

Yet, the underlying message of command and necessity of military order are present: two soldiers are saluting General Washington, one in the immediate foreground and one from the side of the moving column. Most of the men gaze directly forward, off the edge of the painting,

This statue of George Washington at Valley Forge, considered the most accurate of all, is a Gorham Manufacturing Company-casted copy of the one sculpted by Jean-Antoine Houdon that resides in the Virginia State Capitol in Richmond. Permission was granted by the General Assembly of Virginia in 1910 to Gorham to make copies. (psg)

March to Valley Forge,
Trego (moar)

while Washington gazes across the column. More words come to mind.

Survival. Resolve. Discipline. Stubbornness.

A small section at the bottom right of the painting shows the footprints of soldiers unseen. One can guess they were made by the column in front of this one. Those men are headed toward Valley Forge down the Gulph Road. In the upcoming winter cantonment, the men who were the subjects of Trego's painting, the actual flesh and blood that endured a hellish march such as this, would be transformed from a motley collection of citizen-soldiers into a trained military force. Through months of hardship, an iron resolve would be formed, dare we say, hammered, at Valley Forge into a hard core that would see the American Revolution through to a successful end.

As one continues to peer at this painting, General Washington's gaze is focused forward and slightly downward at the men who have pledged their lives to follow him in the dream of American independence. At the same time, his vision is toward the future, in the same path that his men are slowly headed. Even his horse, casually watching the humans passing by, is pointed in that direction. The painting brings a few more words to mind.

William Trego, here in his studio in 1893, was snubbed by the Pennsylvania Academy of the Fine Arts for his Valley Forge painting. In an Academy-sponsored contest, Trego won third place for the painting, although judges declined to offer first- or second-place prizes, making Trego's painting, *de facto*, the best in the competition even though he was deprived of the prize money. (wc)

Future. Chance. Alive. Possibility.

What transpired in the hills of Pennsylvania, a colony founded as a haven for peaceful existence, would be truly remarkable. Valley Forge would be a haven for the Continental army, although many a soldier would view the time spent there in other more colorful words. The transformation that occurred during this harsh winter respite would be crucial to the cause. Trego's painting hints for the keen observer a few last words:

Valley Forge. Final Victory. Independence.

Truly, that was the winter that won the war.

"I can assure these gentlemen that it is a much easier and less distressing thing to draw remonstrance in a comfortable room than to occupy a cold bleak hill, and sleep under frost and snow, without clothes or blankets . . . ."

However, although they seem to have little feeling for the naked and distressed soldiers, I feel superabundantly for them, and from my soul I pity their miseries, which are neither in my power to relieve or prevent."

— *Gen. George Washington*
communique to Congress

Prologue

April 1775 – December 1777

975 days or 23,400 hours.

Those numbers depict the passage of time between the first shots of the American Revolution, fired in the Massachusetts countryside around the towns of Lexington and Concord, and the Continental Army's march into Valley Forge, Pennsylvania, for their winter encampment.

Put in writing, those numbers stand out. To the men and women who pined for American independence, the difference in days and years seemed like an eternity. Beginning that spring day in 1775, the colonial militia and minutemen of Massachusetts, sprinkled with native sons of Connecticut, Maine, and New Hampshire, thwarted the British expedition to capture military supplies and drove the redcoats back to the environs of Boston. A siege ensued approximately eleven months later, and on March 17, 1776, the British evacuated Boston and sailed to Nova Scotia.

General George Washington, the tall, robust Virginian, was chosen by the Continental Congress to head the proclaimed Continental Army, the title proposed by that political body to reinforce that the rebellion was by all thirteen colonies and not just a regional revolt. Washington knew that the British would be back to suppress the rebellion in King George III's

"I wish I could tell you I was coming home to see you, instead I am going to build me a House in the Woods."
— Jedediah Huntington, Continental soldier (cm)

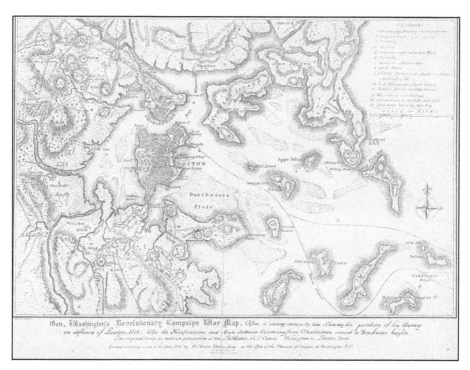

When the British evacuated Boston on March 17, 1776, there was rejoicing in the colonies. However, George Washington knew the enemy would be back, and he turned his focus to discovering where the British would turn up next. (nypl)

North American colonies. Surveying a map of the eastern seaboard, Washington quickly focused his military eye on the city and harbor of New York. Already known to be the home of a large loyal population to the British crown, the rivers that shaped Long Island penetrated deep into the American interior and could serve an invading force looking to cut off New England from the rest of the colonies.

Washington would shift his forces there. In fact, he had sent one of his most experienced general officers, General Charles Lee, to begin construction of defensive fortifications. Unfortunately, little headway on fortifying the surrounding area had been made and the inexperienced Continental Army, buttressed by militia from various states, would be undone by the coming British onslaught.

Licking their wounds, salving their pride, and gathering strength, the British war machine soon unleashed the largest fleet and force ever seen in the western hemisphere, aiming this behemoth at New York City. This joint navy and army operation made quick work of the Continental Army at the battles of Long Island, Brooklyn, Jamaica Pass, and White Plains. The coup d'état was. the capture of Fort Washington, the last American stronghold toehold on Long Island.

Deftly maneuvering and evacuating his command from several difficult situations, Washington hurried his beleaguered troops through New Jersey. After the retreat, the burgeoning American pamphleteer Thomas Paine wrote in The American Crisis, "These are the times that try men's souls." The light of American Independence seemed to be shuttering dark.

Then came the quick strikes at Trenton and Princeton in New Jersey. On December 26, 1776, Washington's wily Continental Army traversed an ice-choked Delaware River on Christmas night and overcame a force of Hessians, the German mercenaries hired by the British crown to augment its army, at Trenton. Eight days later, Washington won another victory at Princeton. These twin successes helped to stave off the threat to American independence and kept alight the hope of eventual victory.

Colonists initially did not blame King George III, the British monarch (above), for the division between the colonies and Great Britain, which colonists believed was caused by Parliament. The king's rejection of a colonial petition and decision to peruse a military solution set the stage to match the colonists in open warfare. (psg)

Although the original plan Washington envisioned called for a strike on New Brunswick, New Jersey, a pivotal British supply depot, the Virginian knew that his army could not continue the campaign past Princeton. With British General Lord Charles Cornwallis' command quickly approaching, the absence of fresh troops to spearhead an assault, and the fact that the Continental Army had been in combat or on the march for several days, Washington decided to call a quick conference of his general officers. The officers elected to head toward safety.

Crossing the Millstone River and destroying the bridge behind them, Washington's men reached present-day Millstone late in the night of January 3, 1777. The army continued the march to Pluckemin, New Jersey, the following day, taking the Sabbath, January 5, to rest in camp.

The Continental Army then marched to the

environs of Morristown, New Jersey, a strategically important town with roads running both north-south and east-west snuggled behind the imposing Watchung Mountains. The Continental Army, numbering around 2,500 men, entered the town of approximately 250 residents on January 6. "At 5 p.m. and encamped in the woods, snow covered the ground" was how one Continental Army officer remembered it. The officers and men found lodgings throughout the small town and surrounding area, while Washington made his headquarters at Jacob Arnold's Tavern, a small establishment on the Morristown Green, at the center of the town.

A view of the statues guarding the Trenton Battle Monument. The victory there on December 26, 1776, revived American prospects after a series of defeats and retreats. (psg)

Morristown was described as "a very Clever little village, situated in a most beautiful vally at the foot of 5 mountains" in a letter from the American encampment dated May 12, 1777. Within this "Clever little village," which boasted between 50 to 60 buildings, including nine grist mills, eight iron forges, seven taverns, and two churches, came one of the cleverest decisions Washington made during the entire conflict: mandating that the Continental Army undergo a mass inoculation for smallpox. An epidemic of smallpox that swept through Morristown most likely influenced Washington's thinking.

The procedure of inoculation was simple in the 18th century. A physician made an incision in an infected individual and then took the same sharp instrument and inserted it under the skin of a healthy individual's arm. This person, in theory, then contracted the disease and through a period of quarantine would suffer a minor case of smallpox. When the soldier regained his health, he would then be immune. Washington himself had contracted the dreaded smallpox virus on a trip to Barbados in 1759 and was thus already immune. As a result, less than two percent of the soldiers inoculated with a strand of smallpox succumbed to either that strand, or the effects of the inoculation that winter. The general also ordered the local populace to be inoculated.

A campaigning season that started with such promise when the British evacuated Boston on March 17, 1776, sunk to the low points of defeat around New York City and the chase across New Jersey during the summer, then turned around with lightning strikes at Trenton and Princeton. Now the year 1777, like the calendar, turned into history with the cause surviving. Coupling the military events with the announcement of the Declaration of Independence in July and the rehabilitation of the Continental Army in Morristown, a glimmer of hope for eventual American victory and independence was on the horizon for 1778.

Continental soldiers, on the march—although depicted in full sets of uniforms, the reality was much different for the rank and file. Many a hard march were in order after Boston. (nypl)

What would this next year bring? Washington, like his counterpart, Sir William Howe, would have to wait until the winter passed and the roads became passable before the next campaigning season could unfold.

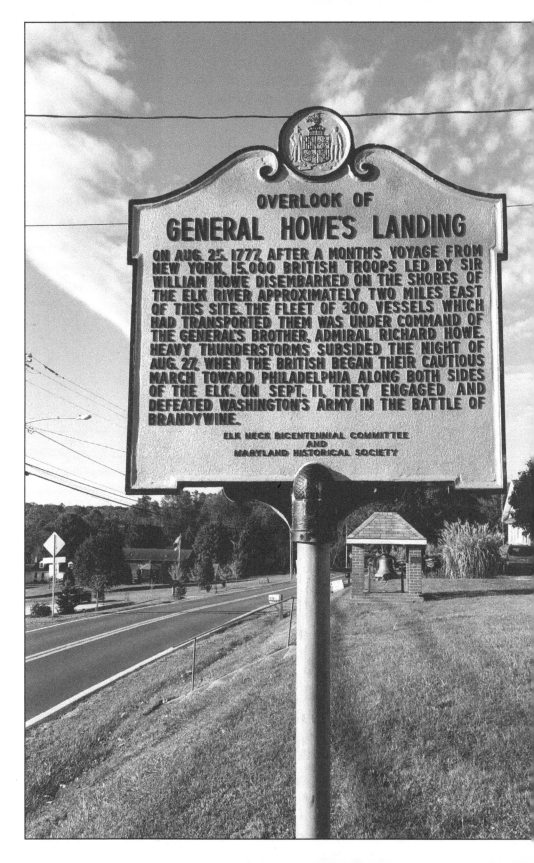

OVERLOOK OF
GENERAL HOWE'S LANDING

ON AUG. 25, 1777, AFTER A MONTH'S VOYAGE FROM NEW YORK, 15,000 BRITISH TROOPS LED BY SIR WILLIAM HOWE DISEMBARKED ON THE SHORES OF THE ELK RIVER APPROXIMATELY TWO MILES EAST OF THIS SITE. THE FLEET OF 300 VESSELS WHICH HAD TRANSPORTED THEM WAS UNDER COMMAND OF THE GENERAL'S BROTHER, ADMIRAL RICHARD HOWE. HEAVY THUNDERSTORMS SUBSIDED THE NIGHT OF AUG. 27, WHEN THE BRITISH BEGAN THEIR CAUTIOUS MARCH TOWARD PHILADELPHIA ALONG BOTH SIDES OF THE ELK. ON SEPT. 11, THEY ENGAGED AND DEFEATED WASHINGTON'S ARMY IN THE BATTLE OF BRANDYWINE.

ELK NECK BICENTENNIAL COMMITTEE
AND
MARYLAND HISTORICAL SOCIETY

To Seek Fortune Elsewhere

CHAPTER ONE
January – June 1777

As the calendar turned from 1776 to 1777, Washington's army was ensconced within the highlands of New Jersey, monitoring the British forces. The British were wintering in upper New Jersey, burrowed into the metropolis of New York City and blanketing the surrounding New York boroughs.

Washington had his army snuggled behind the Watchung Mountains around Morristown, New Jersey, a winter encampment "best calculated of any in this Quarter [of the country] to accomodate and refresh them." By May 1777, Washington's wish of having a respite and reinforcements for his army seemed to have been granted. The Continental army that marched into Morristown on January 6 numbered approximately 2,500 men. Five months later, on May 20, the return for the army showed 38 regiments numbering 8,188 men, with the majority recruited and enlisted for three years or the duration of the war, something Washington had eagerly been pressing upon the Continental Congress and various state governments for a long time.

Around this time Maj. Gen. Henry Knox, Washington's artillery chief, wrote to his wife with an air of hopefulness: "[I]t appears America will have much more reason to hope for a successful

A Maryland historical marker sits atop a bluff and overlooks the location, two miles to the east, where Gen. Sir William Howe's army finally touched Maryland soil on August 25, 1777. (psg)

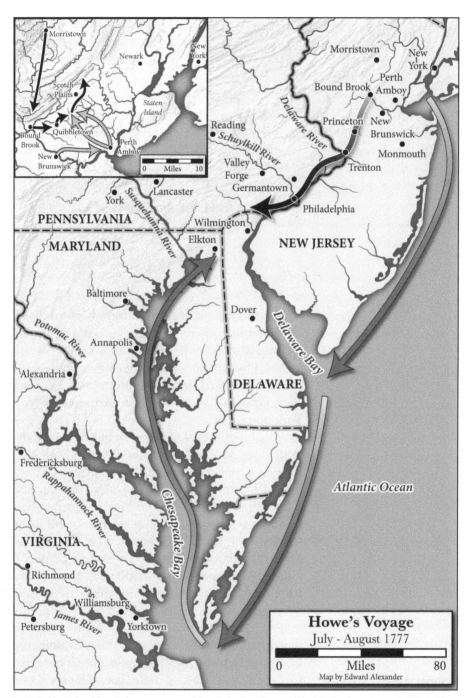

HOWE'S VOYAGE—After being unsuccessful in bringing George Washington's army to battle in New Jersey, Howe embarked his forces for a voyage south, eventually landing on the banks of the Chesapeake Bay and changing the theater of operations for the final months of the campaigning season of 1777. In the ensuing campaign he would successfully capture Philadelphia, the American capital, but ultimately hurt the broader British war effort. (Dark line - Washington's forces / Light line - British)

British ships of war, similar to the one in this painting, transported Howe's army to Maryland. (nypl)

campaign the ensuing summer than she had the last." Arriving from France at this time were much-needed military supplies, including 1,000 barrels of powder, 11,000 gunflints (needed to ignite the firelock of a musket), and even more importantly, 22,000 muskets.

Eight days after receiving the returns for the army, Washington moved his rejuvenated command, marching them 20 miles to the southeast near Bound Brook in the Middlebrook Valley, behind the First Watchung Mountain, the southern of the two Watchung Mountains in the range. Here they were only eight miles from New Brunswick, where a portion of the British army was wintered.

On Friday, June 13, 1777, the behemoth British and German force, numbering 17,000 men, stirred from their winter cantonment. What was transpiring in British-held New York City, with the construction of boats and then transporting them on wagons, suggested Howe's intention to march across New Jersey to strike at the American capital of Philadelphia, a target that the previous December Howe had called off, after Washington's sudden strike at Trenton and follow-up in January at Princeton.

Speculation from both British and American officers and soldiers ran rampant. Washington fully believed that Howe intended to push straight forward through New Jersey in an all-out effort to capture Philadelphia. Captain Friedrich von Munchhausen, of Howe's staff, believed the second

John Sartain painted this likeness of George Washington in 1850, copied from an earlier likeness painted by James Peale. (yale)

Lord Richard Howe, whose nickname was "Black Dick" because of his dark complexion, was brother to Sir William Howe and in charge of transporting the army. (nypl)

day of campaigning, June 14, would see a surprise pre-dawn strike intended to destroy a 2,000-man force at Princeton under American Gen. John Sullivan.

Yet when daylight came on June 14, the action sputtered along with no sense of urgency on the part of the British. In fact, the exact opposite occurred: the British army set up an encampment, a sign contradictory to active campaigning. Or in the words of General Knox, "their conduct [the British] was perplexing." If Sir William Howe was trying to entice the Virginian out of his hillside enclave, he was sorely mistaken, as "Washington is a devil of a fellow, he is back again, in his old position, in the high fortified hills" and did not seem inclined to come down. Even Sullivan's forces had retreated to higher ground from Princeton.

For the next few days, this is exactly where the two forces remained: Howe's men behind temporary earthworks, or redoubts, built around Middlebrook, New Jersey, staring out at

A view from the overlook toward the Elk River. Imagine approximately 250-300 wooden vessels in the water at the top of the image. (psg)

A view back down the Elk River from higher up on the bluff. Ships would have filled the waterway, showing the true might of the British navy in North America. (psg)

Washington's forces positioned in the hillsides of the Watchung Mountains. Skirmishing had been the staple of the preceding days. Since the campaign had opened, the British had not advanced 10 miles, and as June 18, 1777, melted into the history books, both sides geared up for more skirmishing and attempting to discern the other's true intentions. However, as the sun rose the next day, the British army moved, but did not advance, instead retracing its steps to New Brunswick. Three days later the British evacuated New Brunswick.

The British crossed the Raritan River and marched eastward to Perth Amboy with Washington's forces following. Advance attachments, infantry under Gen. Anthony Wayne and Col. Daniel Morgan's riflemen, struck the British rearguard on the Quibbletown Road and at Moncrieff's Bridge. Although it looked like the British were retreating, the wily Howe had accomplished one objective: coaxing Washington out of the highlands and into the more open terrain of central New Jersey.

A sketch of a Hessian soldier, from the time period in which these German mercenaries would have been in the employ of the British crown. (nypl)

Obliged to Leave the Enemy Masters of the Field

CHAPTER TWO

August – September 1777

"For my part, I must say, I would not wish to move until we know with a certainty where the Enemy Intend operating, as we have Certainly for some time past been Marching and Counter Marching to very little purpose" was how one Pennsylvania militiaman explained the current actions of American forces in August 1777. Fellow officers would have agreed with this sentiment, as Howe's army had disappeared into the blue of the Atlantic Ocean.

When the British finally came ashore in northern Maryland, Washington's army was near Philadelphia, having moved to the suburb of Germantown and now encamped along Neshaminy Creek. With news quickly arriving of the British whereabouts, Washington realized that this bit of good news was tempered by the stark realization that no defenses had been constructed between the enemy and Philadelphia. Yet, if he could get to one of the creeks that traversed southeastern Pennsylvania, it could provide an impediment to Howe's approach and force an engagement on his terms.

Washington had to both move his men quickly and also put up a brave front for the

At Paoli, the Paoli Grave Site occupies ground that saw the largest concentration of American dead and wounded. The day after the battle, a farmer, Joseph Cox, made his way to the battlefield and began the interment of "52 brave fellows . . . bury'd . . . next day," although that number would increase by one when the monument was erected in 1817. (psg)

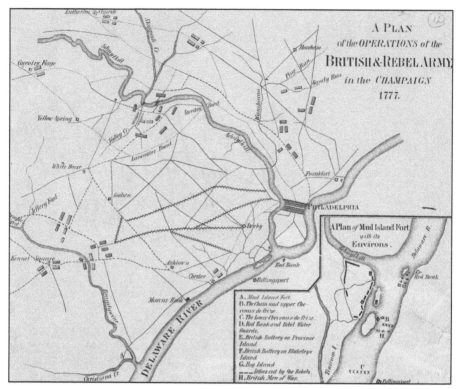

A historic map of the campaign of 1778 shows the operations of the British. It lists the Continental army as the "rebels," which shows the political leanings of the mapmaker. (nypl)

citizenry and the Continental Congress in Philadelphia, so he marched his 11,000-man army, with accompanying artillery and cavalry, through the streets of Philadelphia toward the eventual battlefield at Brandywine.

By early September both forces converged around the area of Brandywine Creek, and skirmishing increased as each side tried to locate the other's main force. On September 9, a heavy skirmish erupted at Cooch's Bridge, Delaware. The next day, Howe was at Kennett Square, 10 miles from Washington's army, which was centered on Chadds Ford.

Howe chose to conduct the coming engagement in his signature style, by ushering in a flanking movement while distracting Washington with diversionary preparations in his immediate front. What ensued on that Thursday was the largest engagement per total of combatants involved, during the entire American Revolutionary War.

Leading a column up the road from Kennett

Square, Gen. Wilhelm von Knyphausen made contact with American troops a few miles from Brandywine Creek. The sparring continued as the American light troops, under Gen. William Maxwell, slowly gave way, the combined British regulars and hired German troops advancing to the creek itself.

Meanwhile, the main British column, with Howe in tow, made a 17-mile, nine-hour march, crossing to the northwest of the American line and appearing on their flank in the early afternoon. Around 4 p.m. the British advanced, routing one American division before encountering stiffer resistance from Gens. James Sullivan's and Adam Stephen's divisions. Mounting British pressure forced the Americans to give way, with one of the notable casualties being the Marquis de Lafayette, who was wounded in the calf.

The battle of Brandywine was the longest and largest engagement of the entire American Revolutionary War. (nypl)

Washington, who had been near Chadds Ford at the center of his line, rushed to the scene and by 6 p.m. had Gen. Nathanael Greene's division and elements of Sullivan's and Stephen's commands south of the town of Dilworth, which was located behind the original center of the American line of that morning. The stand here allowed the rest of the Continental army and accompanying militia to retreat from the field as darkness blanketed the battlefield. American casualties numbered around 1,300 while the British lost close to 600.

Luckily for Washington and his weary men, Howe did not vigorously pursue, which allowed the beaten American army to retreat north across the Schuylkill River. Here, the army was divided: one portion stayed on the west bank of the river to act as a diversion while the remainder marched back toward Germantown.

The Schuylkill was the last barrier between

the British and Philadelphia, and for the next few days the two principal armies shadowboxed as the British crept north. Leaving their encampments around Dilworth (and alerted that Washington had crossed the Schuylkill on September 15), Howe's forces arrived at a major road intersection known as Goshen Friends Meeting House.

Marquis de Lafayette received a bullet wound to the calf during the fighting along Brandywine Creek. However, his service that day continued to cement his role with the army and his place in the good graces of Washington. (nypl)

Washington retraced a portion of his route, moving south down the Lancaster Road and into Goshen Township, dispatching one of his columns toward Goshen Friends Meeting House as well. Continental soldiers, aided by Pennsylvania militia under the command of Gen. Anthony Wayne, formed the left wing and at 2 p.m. they ran into advanced elements of Hessian jaegers, or light infantry, commanded by Capt. Johann Ewald. The Continental attack was initially successful, but the Pennsylvania militia, coming up another road, was met by the main British column under Lord Charles Cornwallis an hour later and was routed from the field.

But fortune smiled on the Americans when a severe thunder and rainstorm rolled in, allowing them to extricate themselves from the valley in which the engagement took place. "An extraordinary thunderstorm" was how Ewald remembered it, "combined with the heaviest downpour in this world." What would become known as the Battle of the Clouds was over, with losses numbering around 100 men for each side. The inclement weather forced the British to camp near the field of battle, while Washington pulled his troops slipping and sliding back across the Schuylkill, leaving behind the 1,500 men of General Wayne's division.

Four days after the deluge that shortened the Battle of the Clouds, Wayne's encamped division was completely surprised in the middle of the night by a British force under Gen. Charles Grey. Wayne's men had been left at Chester, Pennsylvania, to protect both the supply depots and the city of Philadelphia. When the British skirted Wayne's location in pursuit of the main army, the general was supposed to harass and annoy the British by threatening their baggage train, instrumental in eighteenth-century armies to transport extra gear, ammunition, and foodstuffs.

Assuming that he was moving undetected, on the night of September 20 Wayne encamped near Paoli Tavern, a mere four miles from the British bivouac at Tredyffrin. But, unbeknownst to Wayne, spies had located the encampment the previous day when his forces had arrived. Howe instructed Grey to sortie out of the British camp that night, and to keep the element of surprise ordered the men to remove the flints from the muskets, ensuring they could not fire their weapons prematurely. The bayonet would be used freely during the ensuing melee.

The British achieved complete surprise, having a local guide lead them to the site of the American camp. Attacking in three successive waves, Grey's soldiers caused pandemonium in the camp. Wayne's force was completely routed, as was a Maryland

The battle of Paoli monument was erected on September 20, 1877, by the citizens of the local counties of Chester and Delaware. Standing 22.5-feet high, each side has an inscription to read. One line stands out as to the historical memory of the fight in the eyes of the local populace in the nineteenth century: "Sacred to the memory of the Patriots who on this spot fell a sacrifice to British barbarity." The remains of fifty-three soldiers lie in the area. (psg)

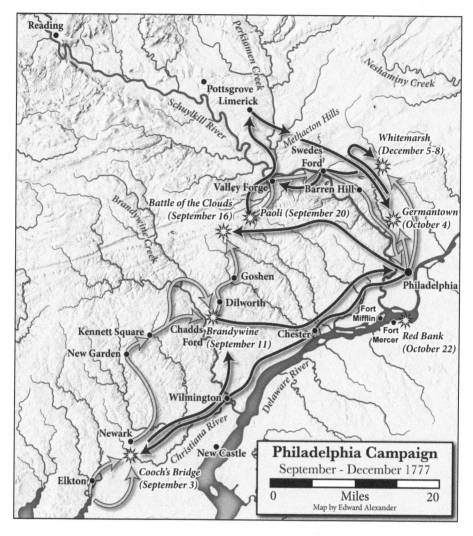

PHILADELPHIA CAMPAIGN—
The theater of operations of the last four months of 1777, which saw Sir William Howe and his British and Hessian forces defeat George Washington's Continentals resulting in the loss of the American capital of Philadelphia, and the eventual winter encampment at Valley Forge.

militia force encamped about a mile away. When morning dawned, Wayne counted more than 200 of his men killed, wounded, or missing, with 71 of the missing among the captured. British casualties came to a paltry four killed and seven wounded.

With the dispersal of Wayne's forces east of the Schuylkill, the British were now masters of the initiative and followed up the action at Paoli by moving toward that waterway. Howe's forces were now an equal distance between the valuable supply depots in Reading and Lancaster and the American capital of Philadelphia. Washington would have to guess which objective was most

Two canon mark the entrance to the grave site at Paoli Battlefield. A stone and lime wall, measuring 65 feet long, 20 feet wide, and approximately four feet high, runs the perimeter of the final resting place of the dead Continental soldiers. During the construction, American Revolutionary War veterans were consulted on how the grave should best be commemorated to give due respect to the fallen. (psg)

enticing to his adversary and plan accordingly. When on September 22 reports reached Howe that Washington decided to protect the precious military supplies at Reading, he reacted by making Washington believe that those targets were in his crosshairs and commenced a short campaign of maneuver.

The ruse worked, keeping Washington committed to protecting his military supplies. Howe then swung to the northeast, sweeping aside fleeing Pennsylvania militia near Swede's Ford on the Schuylkill before marching unopposed into Philadelphia on September 26, 1777.

Although the capital of the rebellious North American colonies had fallen, Washington and his Continental army were still in the field. Once again, was the quest for American independence on the brink of collapse?

One participant remembered "an extraordinary thunderstorm" the day of the engagement. A current historian describes what happened that day as a "classic nor'easter." The battle was abbreviated as the inclement weather ruined gunpowder and cartridges, forcing Washington to choose retreat and to fight another day. (psg)

The Surprize of Germantown

CHAPTER THREE

September – October 1777

Philadelphia was lost. The Continental Congress had rapidly decamped to York by way of Lancaster, Pennsylvania. Washington had chosen to retreat to the west, away from Philadelphia, to protect his vital supply depots instead of defending the capital of the aspiring nation.

On September 16, inclement weather nullified serious action at what would become known as the Battle of the Clouds, and four days later disaster struck at the battle of Paoli. Philadelphia was now in enemy hands.

But Washington kept his forces in the vicinity, situating troops to the north and west of Philadelphia by stationing them around the town of Limerick, Pennsylvania. Deciding after a council of war to monitor the current British configurations, Washington nudged his troops back toward the city to Methacton Hills, a march of approximately 10 miles.

Then luck seemed to swing in Washington's favor. News arrived at his headquarters from a captured enemy courier that the British commander, Sir William Howe, had left a detachment of his command at Germantown, a hamlet outside of Philadelphia. This was the opportunity Washington wanted, the chance to destroy a segment of the British force without entangling himself in an all-out assault on the

At the battle of Germantown, American forces attacked around Cliveden, a home at the center of the battlefield. The Continental army tried several unsuccessful approaches to storm the front door. All resulted in bloody repulses. (psg)

BATTLE OF GERMANTOWN.
ATTACK ON JUDGE CHEW'S HOUSE
From the original Painting in the possession of the Publisher.

Cliveden was the stately home of Benjamin Chew. It was such an iconic landmark of the battlefield that it appeared in lithographs of the battle. (nypl)

entire British army. But he had to act quickly because the longer he waited the more time the British would have to finish erecting fortifications in the area.

And move quickly he did, commanding his army to close on the British and German force, which numbered between 7,000 and 8,000 men. His orders dictated that the army would march in five columns. The center two, comprised of Continental soldiers, would aim for the British camp, attacking the outposts in the process. The two wings, entirely composed of militia from the states of Pennsylvania, Maryland, and New Jersey, would assault the British flanks. The last of the pillars would march down the west bank of the Schuylkill River to distract British sentries posted at one of the ferry locations on that span. Washington was possibly taking a page out of his adversary's playbook.

Characterizing Washington's plan as audacious would be an understatement. Twelve thousand men in five columns on roads separated

between ten to fourteen miles from each other would all be converging at the same time. It was reminiscent of Trenton but with more troops and an additional two prongs.

The march commenced between 6–9 p.m. on October 3. All units were to be in position by 2:00 the next morning, for a two-hour sojourn, and begin the assault the following hour. But when the appointed time came, none of the columns were in place. Yet, just like Trenton, this played positively into the Continental army's hands. The British, made aware of an impending advance by the Americans, had sent out patrols to reconnoiter,

Cliveden defied Henry Knox's boast that he could neutralize it with artillery. Infantry could not break through the British stronghold, either. This helped lead to the defeat of the Americans at Germantown. (psg)

A monument was placed in Germantown to commemorate the action that unfolded in the surrounding area on October 4, 1777. The defeat there would actually have positive implications in the future for the American cause. (psg)

but these returned reporting no enemy sightings. Couple that piece of good luck with the foggy, misty night, and Washington's forces still held the element of surprise.

At 5:30 a.m. the first units moved out and up the hill of Mount Airy, the attack commencing only a half hour beyond the appointed time. When artillery opened fire the British believed they were being attacked by "overwhelming" enemy forces. A portion of the British 40th Regiment of Foot, approximately 120 men, cut off and took refuge in the stone structure of Cliveden.

Unfortunately for the Continental Army that day, Cliveden became a thorn in its side, as artillery and infantry were wasted trying to subdue the fortified dwelling. This combined with the fog, which induced the brigades of Anthony

The monument inscription quotes a letter from Washington to the president of the Continental Congress:

"Upon the whole it may be said that the day was unfortunate rather than injurious. We sustained no material loss. The enemy are nothing the better by the event & our troops, who are not in the least dispirited by it, have gained what all young troops gain by being in actions." (es)

Wayne's and Adam Stephen's divisions to fire friendly volleys into each other, caused the attack on the British and German camps to break down.

Although there were successes for the Americans, including the surprise and rout of British light infantry and a temporary breakthrough in a portion of the British line that netted a few prisoners, the result was the same as many a field fought over by Washington's troops: the general ordered a retreat, but this time with Howe's men in close pursuit. With over 11,000 men engaged, the Americans suffered 152 killed, 521 wounded, and 438 captured; a loss of 10 percent. The British lost 533 combined, with 71 killed, 448 wounded, and 14 missing out of 9,000 engaged, a six-percent casualty rate.

What the numbers didn't show was the

importance of the battle of Germantown in the political and international spheres. Combined with the impressive victory at Saratoga, New York, Germantown showed the French monarchy

and foreign minister that Washington's forces were not defeated and that the loss of the capital of Philadelphia had not hurt the Americans' morale or their ability to wage a successful counter-offensive. The old adage reads, "One can lose the battle, but win the war." Germantown, quite possibly, was that lost battle for the cause of

A battle map graces the front of the Germantown monument. (es)

American independence.

Two weeks after the engagement, Howe recalled his troops from Germantown and consolidated his forces at Philadelphia. The move was strategic, as he sent a portion of his army down both banks of the Delaware River. Two forts there, Fort Mifflin in Pennsylvania and Fort Mercer in New Jersey, impeded traffic on the waterway and hindered the flow of his supplies.

To cover the infantry's advance and to gauge the strength of the American bastion, on October 11 the British commenced bombing Fort Mercer. As this cannonade was taking place, Hessian soldiers landed approximately four miles north of Fort Mercer and prepared to assault the earthworks.

The Hessian commander, Col. Carl von Donop, began his assault on the morning of October 22. To instill a sense of bravado in his men, he informed them that: "Either the fort will be called Fort Donop, or I shall have fallen." Unfortunately for the colonel, his assault failed. The Hessians impaled themselves on the abatis that protected the main section of the fort, and the Americans put up a stout resistance and beat back the assault force, inflicting close to 400 casualties in the process. One of those who fell with a musket ball to the leg, was Colonel von Donop. He would succumb to the wound three days later.

On the river, the British navy also suffered a reversal, as both natural and man-made obstructions in the water thwarted two of the six ships sent to support the infantry. The 64-gun HMS *Augusta* caught fire the next morning and was blown to bits when enemy artillery fire hit the magazine, and the HMS *Merlin* was abandoned by its crew.

George Washington would return to Germantown as president, using the house here during the yellow fever epidemic of 1793 that struck Philadelphia, then capital of the USA. (nypl)

With the attempt to subdue one of the forts by direct assault stymied, the British command decided to continue constructing batteries on Providence Island in the Delaware River. When completed these artillery pieces would join those employed by the British navy to blast Fort Mifflin. The renewed bombardment began in earnest on November 10 and lasted five days. The Americans suffered tremendously, with over 250 of the 400-man garrison becoming casualties. On the night of November 15, Maj. Simeon Thayer left the American flag flying and abandoned the post, slipping across the river to Fort Mercer. Five days later the American commander of Fort Mercer, Col. Christopher Greene, abandoned that post to avoid encirclement and eventual capture by British forces under Lord Cornwallis.

The Delaware River was now open to the British. As a result, George Washington's hope of starving them out of Philadelphia was dashed. Yet, Washington had more pressing matters to attend to following the battle of Germantown. In the coming weeks he would have to decide where to take the army for the upcoming winter.

SITE
OF THE
MARQUEE

ON THIS SPOT GENERAL
GEORGE WASHINGTON
ERECTED HIS CAMPAIGN
TENT (MARQUEE) WHEN
HE ENTERED VALLEY FORGE
DECEMBER 19, 1777.
HE OCCUPIED THIS TENT
UNTIL DECEMBER 24, 1777.
WHEN HE MOVED HIS
HEADQUARTERS TO THE
POTTS HOUSE AT THE
JUNCTION OF VALLEY
CREEK AND SCHUYLKILL
RIVER.

The Army Being Now Come to a Fixed Station

CHAPTER FOUR
November – December 1777

Washington began the latter stages of November casting around for a haven for his men for the approaching winter. Since November 2, the Continental army had encamped at Whitemarsh Camp, around 13 miles from Philadelphia. It was the first permanent location for the army since the engagement at Germantown the previous month.

From this vantage point in the foothills, Washington and Howe conducted the last campaign of 1777. In early December, the British commander marched over 10,000 soldiers from Philadelphia in an attempt to lure the American general out of his defensive works. Minor skirmishing from December 5–8 included an attempted flank movement, a staple of Howe's offensive repertoire, on December 6. But Washington did not budge. Frustrated, Howe began the trek back to Philadelphia after British engineers could not locate a weakness in the enemy lines to exploit. The battle of Whitemarsh was over.

Washington, who had hoped Howe would enlighten him by smashing into his defensive fieldworks, took out his frustrations in a missive to the Continental Congress, detailing his chagrin at the current circumstances, and his preparations for the future. Three days later, after having moved three miles since the battle of Whitemarsh to

A monument marks the site of the bivouac where Washington first encamped when he arrived at Valley Forge. As Washington surveyed the scene, could he even begin to fathom the immense hardships he would need to overcome in the next six months? (psg)

THE WHITEMARSH HEADQUARTERS.

Headquarters of the Continental army at Whitemarsh, the last encampment before Valley Forge. (nypl)

Swede's Ford on the Schuylkill River, Washington's men crossed to the west bank of that river the next day. There they encamped outside of Upper Marion Township at a place referred to as "the Gulph" for a break in the hills that a few soldiers, including diarist Joseph Plumb Martin, would call "remarkable."

This led the commander-in-chief to settle eventually on a winter haven for his army. He finally decided on Valley Forge, 18 miles to the northwest of Philadelphia, thus close enough to keep an eye on British intentions. With densely wooded hillsides to provide cover for the encampment and defenses in case of British advances, Valley Forge also defended the interior of Pennsylvania and the vital supply depots.

"Today we have stormy winds and piercing cold . . .," wrote Reverend Henry Muhlenberg in his diary on December 19, 1777. As the army shuffled up the Gulph Road, seven miles from the previous night's encampment, their destination would be their permanent winter cantonment.

Approximately a year and a half after declaring independence in Pennsylvania's state house in Philadelphia, the Americans lost their capital. (nypl)

From Gulph Mills, where the army slumbered on the night of December 18, the trek took them to the hills of Upper Marion Township and toward another prominence approximately five miles up the road called, ironically, Mount Joy. In the seventeenth century, the 5,000-acre plot of land that was coming into the focus of Washington's army was designated by William Penn for his daughter.

A depiction of the march to Valley Forge invites one to wonder, *Could I have endured that trek in those conditions?* (nypl)

As Washington's men tramped up the Gulph Road and into the rolling terrain that would mark their winter cantonment, they were entering the area known to locals as Valley Forge. The first European inhabitants to claim this part of Pennsylvania came at the turn of the eighteenth century. On October 24, 1701, William Penn granted to his daughter, Letitia Penn Aubrey, and her husband, William Aubrey, over 7,800 acres in entirety. The land that would become so crucial a place of refuge for the Continental army was granted for the miniscule sum of one beaver pelt per year.

Over the ensuing years, the couple had sold off their holdings, and by 1730 the last 175 acres were purchased by a triumvirate of gentlemen: Daniel Walker, Stephen Evans, and Joseph Williams. These three formed the managing trio of the Mount Joy Forge, named for the manor where the Aubreys had resided.

Plymouth Meeting House served as a hospital for Washington's army as they marched to Valley Forge. (psg)

After a few years of operation, the forge became commonly known as "Valley Forge," possibly due to

Plymouth Meeting House, a house of worship since 1708, had a long connection to American history. (psg)

the geographic location the works occupied. The name stuck. Built between December 1742 and April 1751, the ironworks were impressive, having a finery, chafery, bloomery, and splitting mill.

Various early industries popped up around the confluence of Valley Creek and the Schuylkill River in the mid-eighteenth century. Besides the forge that has become synonymous with the military importance of the area, there was a saw mill built between 1751 and 1757 and a grist mill constructed by John Potts, a prominent Quaker ironmaster, in either 1758 or 1759.

Potts's son, Isaac, would build the brick mansion that became Washington's headquarters during that fateful winter. Isaac completed the handsome dwelling in 1770 after two years of construction and continued to maintain a working interest in the grist mill before coming into ownership of it in 1773. Two other sons, Joseph and David, and their cousin Thomas Hackley would ensure the continued operation of the forge by forming the firm of Potts, Hackley & Potts to manage the business.

But the Americans were not the first to

No truer words were recorded about the soldiers at Valley Forge than those inscribed on the archway: "Naked and Starving As They Are We Cannot Enough Admire The Incomparable Patience and Fidelity Of the Soldiery." George Washington wrote these words on February 16, 1778. (psg)

arrive in Valley Forge in 1777. After defeating Washington's army at Brandywine, British forces raided across the Pennsylvania countryside, and a week after the battle, on September 18, the first enemy soldiers arrived in the vicinity. Two days later, more redcoats arrived and began removing all the stockpiled stores, applying a torch to the forge and the other structures in the compound. The only building they spared was the gristmill, possibly out of compassion for the area residents with the approaching winter.

Approximately three months later, another force headed slowly to Valley Forge looking for succor for the coming season. As the American army approached Valley Forge, the Continental Congress slated December 18, 1777 a "public Thanksgiving" to mark the progress in the fight for independence. Washington's men were encamped along the Gulph Road, slowly trekking toward their winter destination when Sgt. Ebenezer Wild of the 1st Massachusetts Regiment recorded the spread of that "public Thanksgiving":

We had but a poor Thanksgiven, Nothing but Fresh beef and Flour to Eate Without aney Salt & but very Scant of that.

There is no better description of the encampment than the names of the two hills that rise over Valley Forge: Mount Misery and Mount Joy. Unfortunately, soldiers would remember more of the former than the latter from their winter in shadow of the hills. (psg)

An 1877 view of the entrenchments at Valley Forge, looking south— 100 years after Washington's men dug these fortifications.
(nypl)

Another soldier, Pvt. Joseph Plumb Martin, was more cynical of the feast of December 18, writing in his diary:

> We had nothing to eat for two or three days previous...but we must now have what Congress said, a sumptuous Thanksgiving to close the year of high living we had now nearly seen brought to a close.

With the approach of the next morning, a Friday, the Continental army finished its march of seven miles down the Gulph Road. Lieutenant Samuel Armstrong of the 8th Massachusetts Regiment recorded that final march of the season to Valley Forge on that sunny, December 19, 1777 day.

> By ten Oclock we to march to a place Call'd Valley Forge being about five or six miles—about Eleven ock we Sit out, but did not arrive there 'till after Sun Sit. During this march we had nothing to Eat or nor to drink.

For the core of the army, these were the final steps of over 200 miles of marching for the campaign season. Armstrong's final line was a precursor for what faced the soldiers that coming winter at Valley Forge.

The majority of the Continental army would

Continental artillery, fortified by earthworks, protected the winter encampment at Valley Forge. Soldiers would have spent hours perfecting this type of earthen defense, in the off-chance of a British attack. (psg)

settle onto the original 7,800 acres that belonged to the Penn and Aubrey families earlier that same century. Washington would rent the Potts's residence from Mrs. Deborah Hewes, a relative of the Potts family who was the tenant at that time. Washington's staff and Mrs. Hewes agreed upon a sum for renting the house, since Continental law forbade mandatory accommodations, in contrast to the despised Quartering Act the British had imposed upon the colonies the previous decade. For £100 in Pennsylvania currency, the Potts's house became the headquarters of the Continental army for the next seven months.

As Washington settled into the Potts's house, his subordinates fanned out for their winter accommodations. Henry Knox, the amiable and rotund chief of artillery, made his quarters adjacent to the Gulph Road, and less than a mile away, William Alexander, Lord Stirling, nestled into his accommodations.

With the general officers finding already-constructed dwellings to call their temporary abodes, the rank-and-file made use of canvas. Tents sprang up as the sound of axes began to ring out across the pastures, fields, and hillsides of Valley Forge.

$\mathcal{H}$ouses in the $\mathcal{W}$oods
CHAPTER FIVE
December 1777 – February 1778

Washington received intelligence that the British were sending a foraging expedition in the direction of Darby, Pennsylvania. He tried to organize a force to counter this enemy detachment and possibly secure the foodstuffs for his own hungry troops. However, the response was startling. According to Brigadier General James Varnum,

> *Three days successively, we have been destitute of bread. Two days we have been intirely without meat. It is not to be had from the commissaries. Whenever we procure beef, it is such a vile quality, as to render it a poor succeedanium for food. The men must be supplied or they can not be commanded. . . the complaints are too ongoing to pass unnoticed. It is with pain that I mention this distress. I know it will make your Excellency unhappy. But if you expect the exertions of virtuous principals while your troops are deprived of the essential necessities of life, your disappointment will be great.*

The Brookside Inn served as the winter residence of the Marquis de Lafayette during his time at Valley Forge. It was possible that a sentry or passerby looking up might have caught a glimpse of the famous Frenchman standing in this second-story window. (psg)

As a result, no response from the Continental army greeted the British expedition. Although not needed, this was another reminder of the dire conditions of his troops on the advent of the winter encampment and Varnum's communication was

The back door of Brig. Gen. James Varnum's winter residence offered a view of the area where his command would have hunkered down. (psg)

a harbinger of the upcoming challenges that winter at Valley Forge would provide for the army commander.

As the army settled into what would become its winter cantonment, Washington's headquarters issued instructions on how the soldiers should construct their winter huts. The wooden abodes would be 14 by 16 feet, each with a fireplace, and lined with 18 inches of clay for insulation. The roofs would also have to be constructed of wood, but no operational sawmills in the immediate area, planking was hard to come by. As an incentive, Washington's orders stipulated a reward of $100 to any soldier under his command who could find a suitable substitute.

General Jedediah Huntington of Connecticut, whose Connecticut Line units arrived from Peekskill, New York, to bolster Washington's forces during the previous campaign season, had the following to say the day after he arrived at Valley Forge.

We are going to work with all our might and Diligence to House the Army in huts at this Place. General Washington seems resolved to concentrate

our army here. Our Men are almost worn out with the constant Marches and Fatigues of the Campaign, but the army is well disposed and will try to make the best of it. I wish I could tell you that I was coming home to see you, instead I am going to build me a House in the Woods.

A soldier graces the top of the New Jersey Brigade monument, peering off into the distance—a gaze many a soldier would have had during the long winter at Valley Forge. (psg)

On Christmas Day, another soldier remarked about the slow progress and the lack of supplies that hindered construction of the winter quarters:

We are now about to build Hutts for shelter this winter Expect in a few days to be comfortable, tho we have nothing convenion to work with - Axes are very scarece - [. . .] we have but one dull ax to build a Logg Hutt When it will be done knows not . . .

As 1777 folded into the history books, the ringing of axes and men yelling, cursing, and joking, could be heard as the encampment began to take shape. The variety of oak trees in the area provided a ready source of wood for the soldiers to build their huts, although construction progressed slowly.

ABOVE: Replica cabins now stand in place of originals. With winter approaching, the originals would have been built in rows as quickly as the men could get the materials. (psg)

RIGHT: This building served as the winter quarters of Lafayette after his recovery from the wound he received at Brandywine and his return to the main army. (psg)

Yet, contrary to popular memory and myth, the winter of 1777-78 was neither overly cold nor ever blasted with blizzard-level snowfall. There was the occasional heavy snowstorm like the one that blanketed the encampment in early February, but unlike the following winter, surviving accounts point toward a normal winter season typical of that part of Pennsylvania. Some days they marked as being pleasant, while another entry marked a different day as "exceedingly snowy," showing the unpredictability of winter. Yet another soldier remarked that rain pelted the encampment on another day, revealing the lack of insulation between the roughhewn timbers that comprised the roof, as an unfortunate junior officer found out when water pooled on the floor over his "shoetops."

Huts sprang up across the vales and valley as the soldiery made the best of their living conditions. When completed, the camp would house close to 14,000 soldiers, equal to half the population of the largest city in the colonies. Army surgeon Ebenezer Crosby put a positive spin on the winter quarters, considering they were racing against the elements, which could set in at any time.

Placards such as this one for Huntington's Brigade mark the various encampment sites. Valley Forge National Historical Park has done a great job researching where the units hunkered down for the winter. (psg)

> *This Log-City, part of which is as regular as Philadelphia, affords much better quarters than you would imagine, if you consider the materials, season, & hurry with which it was built.*

Another army surgeon, Albigence Waldo of Connecticut, penned the following thought six days after the New Year: "We have got our Huts to be very comfortable and feel ourselves very happy in them." Within one month of the army's arrival, more than 2,000 huts were constructed, with each housing between eight and 12 men minus the junior line officers, whose lodgings were more personal.

According to Washington's General Orders of December 18, the layout of the various units' huts was as follows: one hut for every 12 non-commissioned officers and men all in a line. Behind that, one hut to every "General Officer, one to the Staff of each brigade, one to the field officers of each regiment, one to the commissioned officers of two companies."

Although the huts were nearing completion, the suffering did not abate. Being that skilled hands did not make up every squad, many of the cabins were not well insulated nor had they the best ventilation. Borrowing again from the diary of Albigence Waldo, one can feel the agony of the common soldier during those bleak months of winter:

A view across Valley Forge shows the contours of the ground. This was one of the reasons the area was picked. As well as being defendable, the topography could also hide the conditions of the army from prying eyes. (psg)

Poor food—hard lodging—cold weather—fatigue—nasty clothes—nasty cookery—vomit half my time—smoke out of my senses—the devil's in it—I can't endure it . . . There comes a bowl of beef soup—full of burnt leaves and dirt, sickish enough to make a Hector spew . . . There comes a soldier, his bare feet are seen through his worn-out shoes, his legs nearly naked from the tattered remains of any only pair of stockings; his breeches not sufficient to cover his nakedness; his shirt hanging in strings; his hair disheveled; his face meager; his whole appearance pictures a person forsaken and discouraged.

The completion of permanent winter quarters solved only one of the many issues that would plague Washington's army. At one point, one of every four soldiers—3,000 out of approximately 12,000 men—lacked the essentials of clothing. These included shoes, socks or stockings, and coats. The half-naked soldiery presented a stark reality for anyone visiting the encampment. Following a short stay in early February, Gouverneur Morris, a congressman from New York, wrote to friend and fellow patriot, John Jay, that the conditions of the Valley Forge encampment were of a "skeleton of an army. . .a naked condition, out of health, out of spirits."

The clothing shortage even affected the sick and infirm. Clothing disappeared when soldiers were admitted to the hospitals, and convalescents were practically naked. Blankets became scarce as well. To show the depths to which this situation sank Washington had to issue an order stating that a soldier's clothing would be recorded when he entered the hospital, stored properly, and then returned upon the man's discharge from care. If the poor soldier died while in the hospital, his clothing would be given to men returning to their commands or healthy soldiers in dire need.

Even though the conditions were extreme, the bond between soldier and Washington remained rather consistent and high during the time at Valley Forge, as depicted here. (nypl)

Bedding and medical supplies, such as bandages were also in very short supply. Dr. James Craik, who had known George Washington since the French and Indian War, and rose to one of the top surgeon positions in the army, warned the general in the spring: "[I]f I am not, supplied with what I write for [simple medical supplies], it will be impossible for me to give satisfaction here."

American Army at Valley Forge. Soldiers stand guard and try to walk through wintry weather in this depiction of the encampment. The style of quarters show this was before the men had been able to construct permanent winter residences. (nypl)

For approximately 2,000 men the meager supplies came too late. Succumbing to a variety of maladies, ranging from the illnesses that permeated any military encampment of the time to death brought on by hunger and the cold. Few of these soldiers were buried in the confines of the encampment but were interred into the ground near the facilities in which the majority

This view of the cabins shows the composition of the chimneys, which would have kept the approximately 12 enlisted men who occupied the cabins warm throughout the long winter nights. (psg)

of them perished; usually church graveyards that were close to the hospital facilities.

Breaking down the figure of 2,000 deaths, what is not surprising is that most died of disease, which usually killed twice to three-fourths more soldiers than actual enemy-fired missiles. Examining the monthly returns, the startling fact arises that two-thirds of the soldiers succumbed to diseases between March and May, during the warmer months of the Valley Forge encampment. The research shows that the prevalent causes were influenza, typhus, typhoid, and dysentery. Luckily the majority of the army had gone through the smallpox inoculation and a dedicated group of doctors and nurses, including Dr. Craik who lamented the lack of medical supplies, diligently provided care for the suffering soldiers. Otherwise the death toll could have been significantly higher.

The soldier's spirits could be rekindled by food, which also kept his soul and body intact. As one of the maxims passed down from great military leaders of yesteryear paraphrases: "An army marches on its belly." An army also survives a winter encampment with food. Showing his optimism while underscoring the dire need for reorganizing the quartermaster department, Washington ordered the following daily ration for each soldier: one to one-and-a-half pounds of flour or bread, one pound of beef or fish, three-fourths of a pound of pork, one gill of whiskey or spirits. If these amounts could not be supplied sufficiently, then one to one-and-a-half pounds of pork or bacon, one-half pint of peas or beans, and one gill of whiskey or spirits should be given. But most days, the supply did not meet the demand. Diarist Joseph Plumb Martin remembered that he lay "two nights and one day and had not a morsel of anything to eat all the time, save half a small pumpkin."

To further underscore the dire shortage of foodstuffs for the men at Valley Forge, one can view from an excavation in the year 2000 the fauna, or animal, remains of the area of the 1st and 2nd Pennsylvania Brigades. Consisting of approximately 2,000 men combined, at no time during the five-plus months they were encamped at Valley Forge did a soldier get more than one-pound, twenty-ounces of meat or fish. By March 1778, records show the men were eating less than 80 ounces of meat or fish per day.

At one point during the encampment, Washington received a report that the entire supply of foodstuffs was 90 head of cattle and 560 barrels of flour, with the deputy commissary of issues unsure when or if any supplies would be forthcoming. "No bread, no soldier" or "No meat, no soldier" were the cries that rang out across the snowy landscape of Valley Forge. The fate of these men preyed on General Washington's psyche, and the Virginian cast about with all the power at his disposal to correct this issue before the soldiers took drastic measures to correct it themselves. In this time of crisis, he leaned on a stalwart supporter, and the result would be another reason Valley Forge was the winter that won the war.

Not Aware of the Confidence the Army Places

CHAPTER SIX
December 1777 – June 1778

The creak of leather shoes on wooden floorboards; the sighs as the realization of another long night by candlelight has set in; the rise and fall of voices coming and going, echoing throughout the stone house near Valley Creek— these were common occurrences as George Washington haggled, pleaded, requested, and jockeyed with fellow officers, the Continental Congress, and his own rigid decorum to keep his army—the Continental army—intact and ready for active campaigning.

Inside the house, much like inside the story of Valley Forge, lay another level of the importance of this winter in the eventual victory of American independence. The late historian Thomas Fleming called it "the secret war" at Valley Forge. Later generations would name this type "soft war" or even in the twentieth century, "cold war." No shots were fired, no lives were lost on a battlefield, but the fate of thousands rested in the back-and-forth of letters, dialogue, intrigue, and decision-making that raced between Valley Forge and York and Lancaster, Pennsylvania where the Continental Congress and the Pennsylvania government had fled after the fall of Philadelphia.

The latter even questioned Washington's

The headquarters flag signified Washington was in residence. It's now used by the National Park Service to alert visitors that the Potts House is open for touring. (psg)

War Comes to Valley Forge
The British Raid

Before the Continental army arrived, British soldiers descended on the area around Valley Forge, taking supplies. A small skirmish erupted as a result. Although it would be the only fighting to take place at Valley Forge, the local inhabitants would soon grow accustomed to men in uniform. (psg)

decision to seek winter quarters instead of renewing the fight for Philadelphia. One can almost see the expression on the Virginian's face when he opened that communique and then peered out the window of the Pottss house, his measured response showing the underlying concern for and empathy with his suffering soldiers while thinly veiling his frustration at the politicians of the Keystone State.

> *I can assure those gentlemen, that it is a much easier and less distressing thing to draw remonstrances in a comfortable room by a good fireside than to occupy a cold bleak hill and sleep under frost and snow without clothes or blankets. However, although they seem to have little feeling for the naked, distressed soldiers, I feel superabundantly for them and from my soul pity those miseries which it is neither in my power to relieve or prevent.*

Like the wavering glow of the candle on his writing desk, the survival of America also sputtered during those dreary months. The same man who continued to scribble quill

The Isaac Potts House, utilized by Washington and his staff as their headquarters for the winter of 1777-78, was also where Martha Washington stayed when she came during the winter. (psg)

LEFT: Another view of the Potts House through the foliage, capturing the setting sun. Many believed that the time at Valley Forge would prove the setting or rising of fortunes, depending on optimism or pessimism, for the American cause and the Continental army. (psg)

to paper, though, ensured that a chance still flickered through.

Imagine having an army that cried out, "no bread, no soldier" and had resorted to eating bark, boiling leather, and licking rocks out of improvised soup, then having to filter your communication to the Continental Congress for fear that word would leak out to the enemy how awful conditions currently were for the Continental army. Yet that letter, when read by the Congress, would be answered with an incredulous reply, implying that

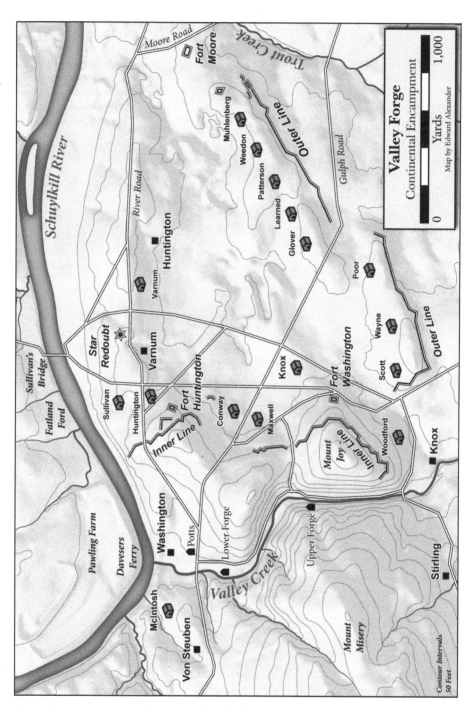

VALLEY FORGE ENCAMPMENT—For six months, Washington's army sprawled across the landscape at Valley Forge, with the various brigades assigned designated spots to erect their winter abodes. General officers hunkered down in private dwellings.

to them, the conditions seemed bleak but not that pitiful. Frustration might not be adequate enough to describe the travails Washington must have mentally endured with this type of back-and-forth.

To compound his exasperation, supplies were plentiful in the local countryside, and even in supply depots scattered throughout the mid-Atlantic region of the colonies. However, transportation—horses and mules and wagons—were scarce, and good foodstuffs rotted in warehouses for lack of means to transport them to where desperate soldiers starved.

The astute Virginian was even ready for the congressional delegation that had come to "rap a demigod over the knuckles," in the words of one of them. Instead, Washington, with serious help from Alexander Hamilton, had a 16,000-word document prepared outlining the current problems with the quartermaster and commissary departments, which he blamed on Congress. After the evening meal, Washington took a stroll with one of the delegates, Francis Dana, and bluntly stated, "Mr. Dana—Congress does not trust me. I cannot continue thus," which was akin to suggesting that his services could be

Being a farmer himself, Washington would have respected the impressive barn and stable. He was always interested in how people conducted their agricultural business and infrastructure. (psg)

Washington used this doorway to take leave of his headquarters. As he descended into the outdoors, one must wonder if he thought about what awaited him that particular day during the winter that won the war. (psg)

lost. This personal touch persuaded Dana into the pro-Virginian's camp and showed itself when voting took place back in Congress. Washington was already showing the gifts of political persuasion that would see him through his presidency in the years to come.

The stable and barn of the Potts House today serves as a small exhibit area. (psg)

He would need this political astuteness throughout the long winter at Valley Forge. Comprising a loose conglomerate of disaffected officers critical of Washington, what has come down in history as the "Conway Cabal," labeled that by later historians, used as their focal point the promotion of Gen. Horatio Gates to replace him. The movement started after Gates's victory at Saratoga in October 1777, when he bypassed Washington, the general-in-chief, and sent news of the victory directly to Congress. Washington became aware of this through John Wilkinson, an aide to Gates who was delivering that message. Fortified with spirit, Wilkinson let slip the purpose of his mission and the view of Washington held by other senior officers.

Thomas Conway, one of the disaffected officers whose name would grace the "Cabal," and a brigadier general soon to be appointed by Congress as the inspector general for Washington's army, then wrote a letter to Gates. In this communique, he urged Gates to angle himself to be Washington's replacement. Washington through intermediaries became aware of the damning letter and made that fact known to Conway. Although Conway denied portions of the letter (for instance the wording of "weak general"), he did not deny it existed. Conway submitted his resignation because of the matter, but Congress held it up due to differing opinions of its members regarding Washington's

The Headquarters Bell, in the house when Washington used it as a headquarters, alerted the general, staff, and guests when meals or other important notices needed their attention or presence. (nypl)

continued leadership of the main Continental army. Instead, they pushed through the promotion to inspector general.

Empowered by his promotion and finding that Wilkinson had let the information slip, Conway wrote to Washington and used the plural word "letters" in his belief that more of his correspondence might have been stolen and brought to the Virginian's or others' attention. Instead of providing Conway the upper hand, the astute Washington homed in on the plural "letters" and realized that this was not an isolated incident.

Through his connection with Henry Laurens, president of the Continental Congress, whose son John was an aide to Washington and, like his father, loyal to the general-in-chief, the Virginian

General Thomas Conway gave Washington angst at Valley Forge. Later, historians would name the infamous 'cabal' after him. (nypl)

Washington cared for the common soldier—in this depiction, he's checking on his outposts at Valley Forge. The experience solidified the bond between the rank-and-file and their general. (nypl)

One of the most—if not *the* most—recognizable images of George Washington at Valley Forge, named *The Prayer*. However, it is highly unlikely Washington ever prayed this openly and publicly. (nypl)

became aware of an anonymous letter written about him. In this correspondence, the country at large was blamed for idolizing Washington. When word of this secret letter reached Congress, that body demanded to see the evidence. When Gates and Conway refused, the other generals who had shown dissatisfaction with Washington either stayed silent or professed their sympathies for him. Furthermore, Congress ordered Washington to hold a council in which Gates was required to be present. This reinforced the supremacy of the general-in-chief.

Conway offered his resignation again, and this time Congress accepted it. Thus, through perseverance, astutely dealing with the erratic behavior of the disgruntled generals, his connections in Congress, and openness in all his correspondence with them, Washington navigated a potentially disruptive experience that would have caused in-fighting among the officer corps and further dissolved morale in the encampment. All this happened within the stone walls of the Potts's house and added further credence to how monumental the winter at Valley Forge truly was.

If that was not enough political fighting,

potential backstabbing, and intrigue in one winter, Washington was faced with having to deal with the new members of the "Board of War," a committee organized in 1776 by the Continental Congress. The Board of War was an idea hatched by Congress to create a panel of general officers who would help oversee the conditions of the Continental army, assist George Washington, and report back to them. For Washington's honor, this was a blow, and in a sinister twist, officers who resented the Virginian or held low opinions of him comprised the board. One idea put forth by this board had been removing the position of inspector general from Washington's supervision and naming Conway to fill it.

John Laurens served as Washington's staff officer. His father, Henry Laurens, was president of the Continental Congress during the winter and an ally of Washington's. (nypl)

As the winter continued at Valley Forge, Washington continued to reinforce his leadership and cement his bond with the men suffering under his command. For starters, although ensconced at the Potts's house, which gave him more comfortable winter quarters than the men under his command, Washington remained in the immediate vicinity. This spoke volumes to the men because instead of retreating to a more hospitable clime, Washington was sticking it out with them under the looming gazes of Mount Joy and Mount Misery in Valley Forge.

One of the bright spots of the winter was

A view toward the huts of Washington's guard, the "Life Guards," that bedded down for the winter near the general's headquarters. (psg)

TOP: Robert Hanson Harrison joined Washington's staff in October 1775 and, during the army's time at Valley Forge, was one of the principle writers of the general's correspondence. (nypl)

ABOVE: Tench Tilghman, a member of Washington's staff since August 1776, worked alongside Harrison. Tilghman tackled almost half of the correspondence that came out of Washington's headquarters during the Valley Forge winter. He would be Washington's longest serving aide-de-camp. (nypl)

the arrival of Washington's wife, Martha, on February 10. She would help brighten the long days of the encampment, once by hosting a dinner in honor of Washington on his birthday, February 22. Although many have speculated about the love between the two, Martha traveled every winter of the war to be at George's side. And with everything going on, the Cabal, the Board of War, and the immense administrative tasks associated with the army—Washington planned and supervised and scrutinized every mile of her trip. The hardships of winter travel and the duties that he faced could not force the two apart during these months.

Baron de Kalb, one of the European officers who joined the American cause, summed up the winter for Washington in a letter to Henry Laurens:

I cannot but observe, in justice to General Washington, that he must be a very modest man . . . for forbearing public complaints on that account, that the enemy may not be apprised of our situation and take advantage of it. He will rather suffer in the opinion of the world than hurt his country . . . . He did and does more every day than could be expected from any general in the world in the same circumstances . . . . I think him the only proper person . . . by his natural and acquired capacity, his bravery, good sense, uprightness and honesty, to keep up the spirits of the army and the people, and I look upon him as the sole defender of his country's cause.

For Washington, the attacks that winter hardened his resolve, much like the winter tested the resolve of his soldiers. Both suffered in the interim, both would triumph in the end. In a letter to a friend, Capt. Ezra Seldon of the 1st Connecticut Regiment summarized Washington's importance to the men for the cause in which they suffered:

I am content should they remove almost any General Except his Excellency. . . . [E]ven Congress are not aware of the Confidence The Army Places in him or motions would never have been made for Gates to take Command.

An etching of Washington's headquarters, completed in the 1920s. (nypl)

Alexander Hamilton, nicknamed the "little lion" by Harrison, had almost unmatched energy and skill when it came to military matters, and he was especially crucial to Washington during the Valley Forge winter. However, Hamilton would come to yearn for a position back in the field. (nypl)

Gaining Every Intelligence

CHAPTER SEVEN
December 1777 – June 1778

After George Washington's death on December 14. 1799, Mason Locke Weems, better known as Parson Weems, concocted a story about the honesty of the late great Virginian. Now one of the most accepted fables of early American history is a young George Washington chopping down his father's cherry tree and when asked his now famous response: *"I cannot tell a lie …."*

If it is true that Washington never told a lie, then there were instances where he did not tell the entire truth. As Washington himself said nineteen years before he took the mantle of leadership for the Continental army: "There is nothing more necessary than good intelligence to frustrate a designing enemy."

During his time as commander of the Continental army, he would assign critical funds and painstaking hours to try and become as adept as possible in managing information and overseeing multiple spy rings. The hope was to glean valuable information that could be secreted to him to provide a better picture of the strategic situations he was facing as army commander. Some of this valuable insight would even be withheld from fellow revolutionaries and politicians. Washington's actions prior to and after the Valley Forge encampment showed the true grasp of why espionage and scouting were

The artillery piece stands as a silent sentinel, guarding the countryside against the unknown. Washington spent the winter peering into that void between the armies, trying to glean British intentions and commandeer any supplies from going into Philadelphia. (psg)

critical to any successful military operations. Even during the more sedentary months of the winter encampment, Washington continued to sift through intelligence reports, staying abreast of British activities while also ensuring that news from his own army did not leak into public sources. On the eve of the eventual movement to settle into Valley Forge, he was able to glean the intentions of his adversary, General William Howe and avoid a major engagement.

Cavalry were the proverbial eyes and ears of 18th century armies. Washington used mounted patrols to keep an eye on the British in Philadelphia. (nypl)

With his army ensconced on the environs of Philadelphia in late November 1777, Washington was in dire need of information on British intentions. He turned to Captain Allen McLane, who would also do great service to the cause near the end of the winter encampment. McLane had various contacts within the city limits and utilized civilians passing to and from Philadelphia, interrogating them on what they had witnessed as they conducted whatever business they had in the city.

On November 28, Washington informed McLane that the army needed to know what the British intended to do in the coming days. Washington made it clear to the captain that he would "depend upon you keeping a very good look out upon their line and gaining every intelligence." Information had reached headquarters that the British had moved across the Schuylkill River and intended to strike Wilmington, Delaware. But Washington also calculated that this could be a feint and that the real move would be to strike the American forces before the division under General Nathanael Greene could arrive back with the main army from New Jersey.

McLane responded almost immediately, tapping information from an old friend who had braved the British occupation of Philadelphia. McLane's source reported that even though

British infantry had been ferried across the Schuylkill, the wagons and artillery had remained on the streets of Philadelphia. Without these contingents, Washington's picture of British intentions became clearer.

By December 4, Washington had received multiple intelligence reports of the British move, and these allowed him to be prepared for the strike when it did happen. What ensued was the Battle of White Marsh which sputtered into a series of skirmishes that last for the next three days.

Even with winter curtailing active operations and the respective armies hunkered down for the colder months, Washington continued to utilize spy networks and tap every source of information.

Within the first week of the encampment at Valley Forge the one-year anniversary of the daring and ultra-successful surprise attack on Trenton, followed by the victory at Princeton, New Jersey came to pass. With an active scouting network confirming that the idea the British would not be advancing in force upon his army, Washington turned those intelligence reports into another more audacious winter strike.

Although earthworks surrounded portions of the Valley Forge encampment, Washington could not be completely satisfied that a winter strike would catch his army off-guard. As the winter wore on and the conditions inside the encampment deteriorated, this concern remained constant. (psg)

One of the views inside Washington's headquarters, where intelligence reports were sent, scrutinized, and acted upon. (psg)

Washington wanted to strike at Philadelphia, utilizing forces near Darby, Pennsylvania to imitate the main thrust against the captured capital city. With the eyes of the enemy turned toward the attack from the direction of Darby and the remaining troops moving to cover that retrograde movement of the British soldiery, pre-selected Continental soldiers would make a rush for the northern sector of the British defensive line ringing Philadelphia. Another column would seize the ferry crossing, destroying anything that spanned the Schulykill River and trapping the force with Howe on the west bank and any potential reinforcing column from the city on the opposite side.

If this plan was implemented, the size and audacity would have dwarfed Trenton and Princeton. However, it was not to be. When the army commander discussed the plan with a select few general officers and circulated his

potential offensive as a document through camp, the response was not positive. The risk was not worth the reward in the eyes of his generals. Washington ceded to the majority opinion. Yet, this shows another example of Washington using the means of scouts and spies and that established network during the winter as a cover for offensive operations.

With warmer weather as late spring rapidly faded, Washington again turned to his trusted network of spies and scouts to determine British intentions. News continued to reach headquarters that the British intended to evacuate Philadelphia and journey by land through New Jersey back to the stronghold of New York City. Yet, a premature move on his part could leave Washington unprepared or susceptible to a British offensive and lead to disastrous results. When one startling report arrived on the Virginian's desk an observer could easily sense the perplexity that still existed in the general's mind when he read the line: "our intelligence is too various to reduce their plan to an absolute certainty."

Staff officers would get a respite in this room in Washington's headquarters, but one notices the writing table in the middle, as reports from scouts or informants could arrive at any time. Washington tried to keep most of the valuable intelligence from being seen by too many eyes, though, as it came into his quarters. (psg)

Directives flew from the Potts house to various outlets, Lieutenant Colonel John Laurens instructed McLane to spare "no pains . . . to discover, if possible, the precise movement when the event is to take place and the rout." With the potential of double-crossing spies and turncoats, Washington's staff officer wanted to ensure the army could trust McLane's contacts. James McHenry, another of the aide-de-camps on Washington's staff fired off the following missive to McLane: "No doubt you have properly covered how far you may trust to the intelligence of your spies, and by comparing the different accounts found out the most faithful."

Finally, on June 18, McLane scored a coup when his company of cavalry overwhelmed a British patrol and netted 32 soldiers. From these captives the Pennsylvanian could settle the question whether the British were evacuating his hometown. The answer was yes. This information was passed on to Washington, who 24 hours later would lead the Continental army out of Valley Forge.

With thousands of lives on the line coming out of a transformative winter, a misstep in the initial phase of the campaigning season could undo all the hardship, strife, and training the army had gone through. Popular culture has become fascinated with the espionage activities of the revolutionary era and to a degree, rightfully so. During the days leading up to and through the encampment, the spies and scouts that served Washington and his associates, were another component of why the winter of 1777-1778 was the one that helped win the war.

Although ensconced in the embraces of his mistress and in an elegant residence within the city, General Sir William Howe also looked toward gaining intelligence about what the wily Washington was up to in his winter haven of Valley Forge.

Sir William Howe, Washington's adversary, was also privy to the importance of espionage and intelligence gathering. After the engagement at Germantown, Howe used Loyalists to augment checkpoints along the major thoroughfares to check persons moving to and from Philadelphia. This put a crimp into the spy network of Washington, with one of his top spies informing him that the current situation was akin to "a hawk would a chicken" in terms of his movements being viewed.

The British commander was beset with numerous reports of the size of Washington's forces shivering in the cold at Valley Forge. Much of this was provided by spies carrying supporting documentation of inflated troop numbers and returns. Also included was a fake note outlining the upcoming movements to be made by the Continental army. A double spy, one believed to be a British asset but in actuality an American agent, carried this invaluable intelligence to the British commander. Couple this with the reports of Loyalists who were reporting more truth—desertions, depravations, and sickness from Washington's camp—Howe had a lot of reports to sift through. Or if not him personally, his military staff.

Although his last words have become famous, Nathan Hale's death was a real example of what befell those who were caught behind enemy lines spying and gathering intelligence. (nypl)

With a continued reluctance to campaign in winter, besides the critical opening of the Delaware River for necessary supplies which could support such a military operation, Howe did not venture forth. He used the excuses of a lack of forage and fodder for man and beast under his command and even credited the enemy on their hardening resolve to see the war through. The degree to which the deception and disinformation campaign that Washington oversaw succeeded with cannot be determined fully. However, the use of spies, scouts, and espionage was a factor and kept Washington's forces from being attacked during the vulnerable months of winter at Valley Forge.

Starve—Dissolve— or Disperse

CHAPTER EIGHT
January – June 1778

The cries of the soldiers were not lost on 35-year-old Rhode Island native Maj. Gen. Nathanael Greene. He had once marched in the rank-and-file, but due to a limp had been sent home by the Rhode Island militia because he was not martial enough in military formation. Greene had been given the thankless task of quartermaster general, replacing Gen. Thomas Mifflin, who had resigned and was now one of the voices on the Board of War critical of Washington's generalship.

The reshaping and revitalizing of the lagging quartermaster department began four days after the Continental army arrived at Valley Forge. Washington had requested in writing that members of the Continental Congress visit the camp and witness the dire straits the army was in, and then began planning a solution to the current predicament. In a subsequent letter to Henry Laurens, president of the Continental Congress, Washington bluntly stated the three options that would be available to the army if the supply issue was not resolved posthaste:

I am now convinced beyond a doubt, that unless some great and capital change suddenly takes place in that line this Army must inevitably be reduced to one or other of these three things.

Nathanael Greene gave up a line command, in charge of a division of infantry, to serve as quartermaster general, a thankless but needed position for the army to survive. This image was a copy painting based off Charles Wilson Peale's original. (nypl)

General Thomas Mifflin served as the quartermaster general of the Continental army before Greene took over. (nypl)

Starve—dissolve—or disperse, in order to obtain subsistence in the best manner they can.

Washington concluded that portion of his letter with a disclaimer: "Sir, this is not an exaggerated picture, and that I have abundant reasons to support what I say."

This prompted action. Within a month, at the end of January 1778, the Board of War had formulated their view. These underscored the need to appoint a quartermaster, stating obviously that it was "a Matter of great Importance and immediate Necessity." On January 31, Thomas Jones, serving as deputy commissary of issues and charged with distribution of foodstuffs and supplies, reported to Washington that the entire allotment of food was 90 head of cattle and 560 barrels of flour. For the sake of comparison, if one cow weighed 700 pounds, then 90 head of cattle would weigh 63,000 pounds. Even if the entire animal was indeed edible, with close to 12,000 men in camp on a daily ration of one pound of meat per day, that supply would run out in five days!

Although reluctant to relinquish a field command, partly because of the thankless task and how he would be remembered—"No body ever heard of a quarter Master in History as such or in relating any brilliant Action"—Greene though would consent to accepting the post, especially since George Washington personally wanted him

Due to the mismanagement under Mifflin and a myriad of problems, many a soldier would die during the winter. This one is buried in the cemetery of St. Peter Evangelical Lutheran Church. (psg)

in that position. On March 2, 1778, Congress confirmed his appointment in a resolution. Greene would be joined by two gentlemen he trusted as staff officers, thus ensuring a smooth transition and a powerful trio to begin the vital task of more effectively supplying the Continental army.

John Cox, an eminent Philadelphia merchant, would oversee all purchases and examine the stores. Charles Pettit was tasked with keeping the books and overseeing the cash for the department. Greene would handle the military duties required of the department and order the levels of supply needed and issue them to the army.

What these three men inherited was a quartermaster department that had not had direct oversight since the fall of 1777, when on October 8, Thomas Mifflin placed before Congress his resignation as quartermaster general. His displeasure with Washington had been growing since the reversals during the campaigning year,

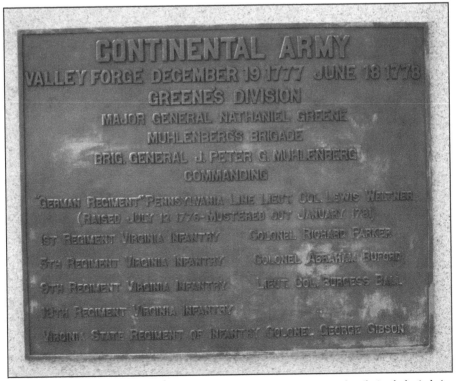

A plaque shows Greene's former command—one he led during the campaign that culminated at the winter encampment of Valley Forge. (psg)

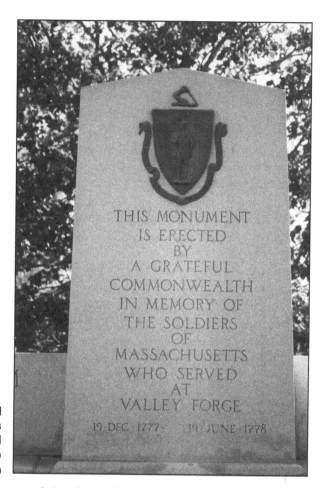

THIS MONUMENT IS ERECTED BY A GRATEFUL COMMONWEALTH IN MEMORY OF THE SOLDIERS OF MASSACHUSETTS WHO SERVED AT VALLEY FORGE 19 DEC 1777 19 JUNE 1778

Greene, as quartermaster, had to supply troops from across the 13 colonies. All would depend on Greene's ability to revive the department. (psg)

and he decided to not inform the general-in-chief of his resignation. Instead he left for home and recuperation in Reading, Pennsylvania. To add to the ridiculousness, Congress dallied on accepting his resignation, which that body finally consented to receive on November 7, almost an entire month after Mifflin had tendered it. If that was not detrimental enough to the cause, Mifflin's behavior was rewarded when he later attained a place on the Board of War. He would continue with the duties, though, until a replacement could be found, but he spent much of his time absent at his estate.

That successor would not be named anytime soon, and instead of providing what assistance he could in the interim, Mifflin let the quartermaster department descend completely into chaos.

Now four months had lapsed before Congress finally named Mifflin's successor. Those who paid the price for this neglect were the huddled masses of soldiers at Valley Forge. The horses that pulled the artillery and wagons, the backbone of any eighteenth-century army, suffered as well. A horse needed 12 pounds of hay and eight pounds of grain a day. By the end of the encampment over 700 horses would perish due to starvation.

In a letter to Henry Laurens, dated March 26, Greene acknowledged the receipt of his appointment and described his dilemma: "I have not received any Returns from General Mifflin, and therefore can only conjecture as to the full Extent of our Wants."

Approximately a week into his new assignment the Rhode Islander had thousands of tools, such as shovels and spades, tomahawks and even cloth used for tents brought to the encampment. These items were essential in improving the overall quality of life for the soldier, especially when active campaigning began again. Most of

As the divisions filed in to the Valley Forge, each would have a designated area. Greene would have been privy to where the different divisions were encamped to fulfill his quartermaster duties. This marker shows the location of General John Sullivan's Division during the winter encampment. (psg)

these items had been collecting dust and mold in various warehouses throughout the immediate colonies.

Nine days after his assignment, Greene was already putting his mark on the department by creating order out of chaos. In a letter to his deputy quartermaster general, Greene ordered him to "minute down every place where you find publick stores, what they are, and in whose hands." In a drastic understatement, Greene concluded, "There has been great losses sustained for want of attention."

Even when supplies had been gathered, "a want of Wagons" caused further headaches for Greene. Prior to his appointment, the state of Pennsylvania had called for the service of 280 wagons for the needs of the state, which had a direct correlation to the Continental army gaining use of these vehicles to haul much-needed supplies. The dearth of wagons became so great that inhabitants in Pennsylvania actually hid theirs to avoid having them impressed by the army. When wagons were available, the reliability of the drivers was suspect. Approximately 30 wagons from one county made one trip to Head of Elk, Maryland, in February 1778, but the drivers then deserted when trying to get across the Schuylkill River. Another group of waggoneers "laid down their loads [of flour] on the Horse Shoe road" and went home with no explanation given. Depreciation of Continental currency exacerbated the problem, much like it did with the purchasing of foodstuffs. Thus, Greene inherited a faulty system of procuring wagons, from difficulty to obtaining them to paying for them. The end result was that food spoiled (when it could be purchased) from want of wheeled transportation, and men and beast suffered.

In another letter, this one addressed to the "Inhabitants of the United States," Greene displayed his public relations savvy in an attempt to explain the past "irregularities" that had taken place within the quartermaster department. He

Washington visited the sick at Valley Forge. Such reminders inspired the general to fight for better supplies and conditions. (nypl)

then promised his leadership would be vastly different:

> *In order to remedy the manifold inconveniences arising from these causes, and, as much as possible, to guard against abuses in future, great care will be taken to engage such persons in the department who are the best adapted to the business of several employments, and the most likely to preserve a proper deportment and to give satisfaction to the well disposed part of the community. . . .*

Like Washington, Greene knew that the problems that plagued the encampment could not be remedied overnight, but he believed they could stop these abuses from happening in the future. Greene, through active oversight, advanced planning, and tighter control of record-keeping, would ensure that Valley Forge would be the start of yet another hopeful transformation. In June

1778, when the army eventually marched out of the winter encampment, the quartermaster department would be ready to supply the troops on active campaign.

This included plans that Greene had implemented within days of his appointment, which started the stockpiling of approximately 800,000 bushels of grain and all the hay his department could attain. The grain and hay would be stored at 15-mile intervals along the northerly route of march that Washington had planned to take for the 1778 campaigning season.

One of the more pleasing tasks that Greene accomplished was finding whiskey and rum in the stores of local sutlers that his commanding general could then distribute to the rank-and-file to celebrate overcoming the difficulties of the winter encampment.

With the hope for the soldiers to be better fed and supplied, another officer rose to the forefront to help train that army. Yet, even Greene played a part in helping this brother officer with his training regimen. With the singing of an alliance with France, the French had provided shipments of arms, with the most coveted being the Charleville musket, named after the armory it was manufactured in beginning in 1717, that fired a .69 caliber lead musket ball. These would provide a uniform standard of arms for the Continental army. Greene, with able assistance from Commissary General Jeremiah Wadsworth, had leased wagons waiting at the wharfs to transport the cargo from ship to encampment.

If Greene became one of the unsung heroes, his brother officer, discussed in the next chapter, occupied the other end of the spectrum. When the army took the field the following spring, Valley Forge would have played a part in their development in that acumen as well.

Anthony Wayne, a native of Pennsylvania, was a brigadier general and acting division commander at Valley Forge. He was one of Washington's most aggressive battle commanders, earning him the sobriquet "Mad" by his soldiers for his bravery and courage under fire. (psg)

The Baron

CHAPTER NINE

February – May 1778

Hailing from the fortress town of Magdeburg in Brandenburg-Prussia, Baron Frederich William Ludolf Gerhard Augustin von Steuben was 47-years old when his horse and sleigh cantered up to the Continental army encampment at Valley Forge. By his side strode a Russian wolfhound, impressive in size, like the Prussian himself. In the Baron's pocket was a letter of introduction to be handed to Gen. George Washington. He was hoping to gain a commission as a major general and thus win the pay that accorded such rank.

His journey to Pennsylvania was circuitous. Von Steuben traveled to Paris, France, in June of 1777 and through connections to the French foreign secretary Charles Gravier, comte de Vergennes and Pierre Beaumarchais, a French arms dealer and author of the play, *The Barber of Seville*, was able to secure a meeting with Benjamin Franklin and Silas Deane. Within a series of meetings, Franklin and Deane, slowly became cordial with the Prussian and helped secure his transport across the Atlantic and introduction to the Continental Congress. Although Franklin and Deane were privy to the fact that von Steuben had never risen to the heights of rank stated in his background, Washington and the Congress were unaware of it. In fact, Baron von Steuben had never risen above the rank of captain in the

Baron von Stueben, made of bronze, stands over eight and a half feet tall—an imposing figure, much like he was to the men of the encampment. (psg)

Baron von Steuben, who became inspector general during the Valley Forge encampment, mixed European military training with American views on soldiering to train the army during the pivotal winter of 1777-78. (nypl)

famous Prussian military of Frederick the Great. In 1771, he received the title of "Baron" from the Prince of Hollenzollern-Hechingen, after serving in that German principality.

What set von Steuben apart in the eyes of the American representatives? His background, as it was widely known that the Prussians had instructed their officer corps to actively promote the emotional and physical well-being of their men. Also widely known was the fact that the Prussian military had the example of Frederick the Great, who as a military leader shared in the hardships of his men and would be seen on the training field lending a hand to tactical drills. Von Steuben had spent time in the rank-and-file gaining his officer commission. These experiences would build the foundation of the rules that he would, with some tweaking to take into consideration the psyche of the American volunteer, use to aid the continued evolution of the Continental army.

None of that mattered in the wintry mix of Valley Forge. What did matter was that this European officer had chosen to serve as a volunteer under Washington. This "ancient God of War," as one soldier described him, would be crucial to the American war effort, second only to Washington himself in that winter that won the war.

His reception at Valley Forge was evidence of the republican virtues of acknowledging dignitaries, as Washington's greeting was subtle and quiet. Four days after Baron von Steuben's arrival, Washington acknowledged him in a letter to the president of the Continental Congress, Henry Laurens. The gears inside the commander-in-chief's head were already churning. Although Washington was coy with his logic, his aide John Laurens, son of the previously mentioned president of Congress, wrote to his father, a fortnight after the Baron's arrival:

A Continental soldier, wearing the attire for one serving in the North. There were not many soldiers that had this entire uniform at Valley Forge. (nypl)

"The General seems to have a very good opinion of him and thinks he might be usefully employed in the office of inspector general."

However, there was intrigue within the American cause. General Thomas Conway, who had overtly tried to unseat Washington as commander, was still the inspector general in February 1778. Yet, the politically astute Washington found a way to sidestep this issue; as Conway was currently serving in Albany, New York, Baron von Steuben was assigned as "acting inspector general."

Peter S. Du Ponceau served as an aide and guide to Stueben—and as his English profanity translator. (nypl)

The die was cast and von Steuben would become the drillmaster. On the exterior he showed all the trappings of a great military leader; "he seemed to me to be the personification of Mars," was how one former foot soldier remembered his first glimpse of the Baron many years later.

In the two weeks since his arrival, the energetic baron had not been idle. To endear himself to the army, he began making rounds in

The plaque on von Steuben's monument shows the general in action on the drill field. (cm)

the encampment and striking up conversations, helped by his dual-language English and French interpreter, Peter Stephen Du Ponceau, who was born Pierre-Etienne du Ponceau. Du Ponceau would translate von Steuben's conversations with the English-speaking officers and enlisted men into French, which was the Baron's second language. Instead of the haughty nature that was reminiscent of the Prussian style, Baron von Steuben connected with the American army with his more candid and rough-edge personality. But underneath this veneer, a sense of shock grew in the Prussian's military mind.

What he witnessed around the log huts and campfires was a motley, ragtag force that styled itself an army. Disorder was rampant in the make-up of the units, as von Steuben noted, "sometimes a regiment was stronger than a brigade. . . regiment consiste[ed] of thirty men and a company of one corporal!" This all underscored Washington's chagrin with the Continental Congress's insistence on short enlistments and dependency on militia to fill the gaps in the regular army.

But where to start was the question foremost in Baron von Steuben's mind. The entire structure seemed to be fumbled. Returns for the size of the Continental Army, which stated who was absent and for what reason, were lacking. Most were filed simply "to the best knowledge and belief" of the various company captains. In another instance that would befuddle military leaders of any century, one regimental commander, when asked how many men he had in his command, replied casually, "Something between two and three hundred men."

The dire manpower situation was summarized in a numbers report dated February 29, 1778. The Continental army counted 22,283 men total, but, of that figure only 7,556 were reported as fit for duty and currently encamped at Valley Forge. At least 3,201 were counted as sick and present, whereas 3,680 were marked sick but absent. Another 3,558 were listed under "on command and extra service" in various capacities. The remaining 1,256 were on furlough. Furthermore, thousands on that list had a note next to their name describing missing articles of clothing, which obviously prohibited their effectiveness.

The men who stared back at Baron von Steuben as he traversed the encampments wore an array of clothing shocked the Prussian. He remarked that one officer attended guard duty on horseback wearing "a dressing gown, made of an old blanket or woolen bedcover." Even the weaponry puzzled him, as some firearms were caked with "rust, half of them without bayonets" and with deteriorating ammunition pouches. Men turned out in the same company with a wide array of muskets, fowling pieces, and rifles, making ammunition resupply a dizzying and taxing enterprise.

Lastly, regulations governing the army while in camp, the structure to assigning guards, and guidelines for marching in column were almost non-existent. The Prussian spied the close resemblance to the British mode, which took much of the responsibility from the officers and placed it on the men in their charge. If the men were stationed for guard duty and the officer was conspicuously absent when the fighting erupted, all other duties were reassigned to the respective sergeants. Baron von Steuben, who trained under

The Baron's steely gaze peers out over the training field at Valley Forge. (cm)

the exacting eye of Frederick the Great, would set about making a change to this as well.

On Thursday, March 19, and approximately one-month after his arrival at Valley Forge, von Steuben ushered in a change that would see the Continental army on its path to eventual victory. Waking up promptly at 3:00 a.m., this master of appearances emerged from his tent resplendent with powdered wig and dressed in his military uniform of old. He lit his pipe, strolled out with papers in hand, mounted his charger, and guided the horse to the parade ground.

With puffs of breath billowing white in the cold early morning dawn, the proud veterans of Washington's army stood drawn up in two lines. Occasionally a foot would stamp, or a body shudder as the men, barely clothed, stood freezing in formation. Toward them came Baron von Steuben, the stranger who some had seen strolling through their encampments and asking a myriad of questions. Now these soldiers would learn who this officer was and why they were standing on the parade ground on that cold spring day.

A "model company" of 100 men from each brigade matched with the 50 Virginians that comprised Washington's headquarters company was what von Steuben saw on the Grand Parade ground that Thursday morning. As one historian describing von Steuben's role at Valley Forge aptly put it: "[O]n that March day, the question of whether it was possible to turn a collection of farmers, landless laborers, tradesmen, and Irish and German immigrants into an army would be settled."

Baron von Steuben quickly got down to business.

Establishing a Uniform System of Useful Maneuvers

CHAPTER TEN

March – May 1778

One of the best testaments to the effectiveness that Baron von Steuben's training regimen had on the Continental army came from an enemy officer, the astute, career junior officer, Capt. Johann Ewald. In charge of a company of *jaegers*, or light infantry, Ewald participated in many engagements during the American Revolutionary War. He recorded the following in his journal in 1778:

> *During these two years, the Americans have trained a great many officers who very often shame and excel our experienced officers. . . . I must admit that when we examined a haversack of the enemy, which contained only two shirts, we also found the most excellent military books translated into their language. . . I exhorted our gentlemen many times to read and emulate these people, who two years before were hunters, lawyers, merchants, physicians, clergymen, tradesmen, innkeepers, shoemakers, and tailors.*

From the foot of the statue of Baron von Steuben, one can look out toward the drill field. (psg)

That was all in the future. Beginning on that fateful March day, von Steuben selected a 20-man squad out of the 150 gathered on the Grand Parade ground that morning. With their rifles stacked, the Baron started from the very beginning, explaining the proper attention pose or, in the parlance of the day, the "position of the soldier."

A depiction of a soldier going through the procedure of loading a musket, which was a 12-part process at the time of the American Revolution. (nypl)

As the Baron read from his notes in his stentorian voice, the orders were translated and the model mini-company quickly gained the right posture, feet placement, and gaze. Then von Steuben himself acted out the order, and in those few moments a bond began, as humor in the strutting, standing, and cursing that came from the German wrinkled through the gathered soldiers.

When something went amiss, the Baron would call over Du Ponceau and instruct him: "My dear Duponceau. . .come and swear for me in English, these fellows won't do what I bid them."

The Baron also quickly learned an English curse word that his booming voice would echo out across the field when his temper boiled over.

With the soldiers in the right stance, he next taught them how to dress their ranks—turning their heads, darting their eyes right and left, and perfecting alignment on their neighboring comrade. With the ranks to his liking, the Baron taught the "common step," the route of march for consistency, which equaled 75 steps a minute and covered exactly 28 inches in movement. Soon the constant tramp, tramp, tramp, of the soldiers' heels could be heard around the parade ground, and this progressed into the other quicker steps of the various marches.

Next came the tricky part of turning—90 degrees to the right and left--, and then the more difficult "about face" command, which constituted a 180-degree change in direction. After completing all these maneuvers and new directions, von Steuben dismissed the men. This first lesson had lasted approximately an hour.

After lunch, the model company reconvened. Broken into squads, the men quickly reviewed the morning lessons and then implemented new procedures. This organization of training and planning became the regimen as the days unfolded: new lessons implemented in the morning, reviewed after noontime, and then another set of regulations, movements, and orders instructed in the afternoon before von Steuben dismissed the men for the day.

With the drudgery of a static winter encampment, von Steuben's drill exercises naturally attracted the attention of other soldiers who would gaze from the fringes of the parade ground. The ever-intuitive German used the onlookers as a teaching tool to boost morale and stress the importance of the military lessons he imparted. With an audience to showcase the new military arts, the model company could take pride in what it was undertaking daily.

A 1934 sketch of von Steuben drilling the soldiers shows the personal, hands-on training the baron initiated. Melding European methods of drilling to fit the personality of the volunteer American soldier led to diversified training techniques. (nypl)

After five days of training, von Steuben, through his temperament—a mixture of fits of rage, humor, stoicism, and military decorum—and the men had come to like each other. The Baron came to understand the Americans' psyche, and the American foot soldier learned his craft. George Washington was impressed and ordered March 24, 1778, as the day the entire army would start learning from the Baron's model company.

Thus, at 9:00 a.m. on the appointed day, the brigades were lined up in their respective brigade encampments' parade grounds (the open space near their huts) to "begin their exercise, each regiment on its own parade."

To implement the training, Washington began forming a properly functioning office of inspector general while excluding mention of Thomas Conway, who had been given that position by the Continental Congress. Washington's go-around of this sticky situation

On this field soldiers practiced drill under the direction and gaze of von Steuben. (psg)

came as Conway's resignation was about to be accepted by Congress. Furthermore, the general-in-chief instructed each brigade commander to nominate an officer to serve as the inspector general for his respective command. These officers would serve von Steuben as his assistants and de-facto eyes and ears during the upcoming training. Four officers would act as sub-inspectors to oversee the above-mentioned inspectors and monitor larger formation drills. The officers picked were Col. William Davis of Virginia, Col. Francis Barber of New Jersey, Col. John Brooks of Massachusetts, and Col. Jean-Baptiste Ternant, a Frenchman.

Although not sanctioned by Congress, on March 28, Washington made von Steuben's position official when he issued the following circular:

Soldiers not participating in von Steuben's drills passed the time watching those training in the maneuvers from the fringes of this field, providing commentary when an error was made. (psg)

Baron Steuben, a Lieutenant General in Foreign Service and a Gentleman of great military Experience having obligingly undertaken to exercise the office of Inspector General in this Army, The Commander in Chief 'til the pleasure of Congress shall be known desires he may be respected and obeyed as such.

Over the next month, the Continental army drilled. The diarist Joseph Plumb Martin referred to this period as one "continual drill," but the overall reaction was more positive than negative. Like a good professor, von Steuben had developed a syllabus in which his training would be passed on to sub-inspectors and the selected brigade instructors. In turn, these men would select a 20-man squad from each brigade. Furthermore, every captain in command of a company of infantry would train a squad of like-numbered men, until every soldier had received the basics of this training and drill.

When proficient in small-unit maneuvers, the men would drill in larger formations. No one was exempt from this new training regimen; even officers of higher grade participated, a break from the British model of military drill. In the afternoon, the grade officers—from majors to captains to lieutenants—would go over the drill themselves, providing entertainment to the rank-and-file as their superiors fumbled while learning their charges' roles. From setting the example to insisting that training stayed current, the Baron demanded that the officers were responsible for their men. This important fact was not overlooked and was practiced by von Steuben himself, as John Laurens expressed: "The Officers in general seem to entertain a high opinion of him, and he sets them an excellent example in descending to the functions of a drill-Serjeant."

Baron von Steuben drilled a squad in front of Washington's headquarters to show off their newfound discipline. The review gave the commander confidence that the soldiers marching out of Valley Forge would be vastly different than the ones who had shuffled in. (nypl)

Progress was evident. Within three weeks, entire regiments could train together instead of the company-by-company instruction that had been the standard. The goal was to have the entire army able to maneuver and form for combat as a single entity. This positivity infected each level of rank, and although most of the soldiers and officers had been on active duty for at least a year, the drill and training actually made them feel like soldiers able to stand up to the British and match them maneuver for maneuver. Time would tell, however, if this would hold true on the battlefield.

To expedite the training, von Steuben eschewed the traditional manual of exercise, which taught the soldiers how handle their muskets. Instead, the German went straight to

A look across the breadth of the encampment area is just one section of the entire area used by the army. None of the trees on the horizon would have been there by spring 1778, as wood was used for the huts and also to try and keep warm. (psg)

executing the maneuvers and marching from the select squads to battalion composition to the larger brigade formations, implementing the standards of the "Manual of Exercise" along the way. By doing this, von Steuben took into consideration the psyche of the American soldier, a volunteer who had a basic handle on firearms but needed to learn the more practical aspects of soldiering.

Having already completed the rudiments of marching within three weeks of the training, von Steuben had entire regiments drilling together without the benefit of fifes and drums to mark the changes of pace. By mid-April, the regiments were moving from column to line formations, mimicking going from the march into line of battle.

Then momentous news arrived in Valley Forge. On the first day of May, word reached the encampment that France had agreed to a military alliance with the fledgling United States. Washington quickly landed on the idea of a review of the army to highlight the training just completed under von Steuben's guidance and to showcase for their new allies their military acumen.

Titled the Grand Review, the military exercise, took place on May 6, 1778, and was a grand success. Baron von Steuben's training was evident in every movement, maneuver, and firing drill that the men performed. As John Laurens would write after that May day: "The order with which the whole was conducted, the beautiful effect of the running fire which was executed to perfection, the martial appearance of the Troops, gave sensible pleasure to every one present."

Within two weeks of the Grand Review, a portion of Washington's army would have their chance to test every aspect of the Baron's drill in live action.

Here are the English in Earnest

CHAPTER ELEVEN
September 1777 – June 1778

September 26, 1777, was a pivotal day for Philadelphians. For those supporting the cause of American independence, that early autumn day marked the beginning of the British occupation—a time of dread, fear, and hiding. For those metropolitans of America's largest city supporting King George III, termed "Loyalists," watching British troops marching onto Second Street and turning up Vine Street, the day was one of euphoria.

The British quickly moved to solidify their gain and prepare for the upcoming winter season. By the end of November, British and Hessian forces had captured the forts south of the city on the Delaware River, allowing for foodstuffs and supplies to be unloaded in the city wharves. The cornucopia that materialized in Philadelphia in the first weeks of the British occupation was a stark difference between what would be endured by Washington's men during the winter months ahead, even though, naturally, there would be shortages for soldiers to gripe about in the British encampment as well.

Howe's men also went about constructing earthworks around the perimeter of the city to defend against any possible motives

As he and his men shivered outside Philadelphia, George Washington might little have imagined he would one day return to the city at president of a new nation made possible by his army's sacrifices. Washington's statue now stands outside Independence Hall. (cm)

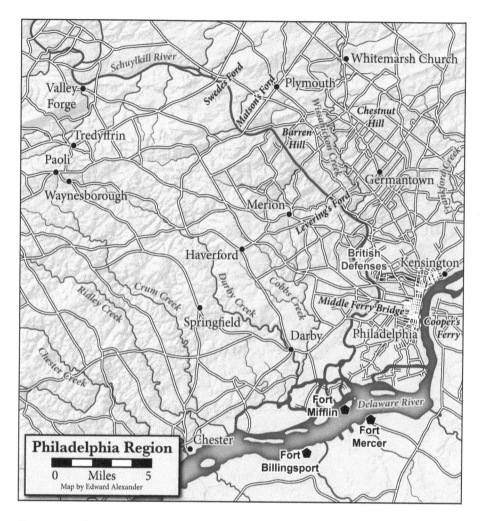

PHILADELPHIA REGION—A view of the surrounding area of Philadelphia, Pennsylvania depicting the British defenses, including the forts that guarded the Delaware River. The capture of the forts was vital to the supply of the British and Hessian forces wintering around the city. Other town names and places that were prominent during the 1777-78 winter are highlighted on the map as well.

from Washington. As mentioned previously, Washington had struck a detachment of British troops garrisoning Germantown outside the city.

British and Hessian troops' daily rations consisted of three-quarters of a pound of beef, a pound of wheat flour for bread, and rice, peas, and vinegar doled out weekly. To complement these army foodstuffs, any soldier or officer with money jingling in his pockets had fresh food options that arrived from the Pennsylvania countryside, showing that hard currency was more a motivating factor than political allegiances as well as dispelling the myth that the Valley Forge winter was destitute for civilians around Philadelphia.

Sir William Howe moved quickly to establish an aura of permanency by the British on the city. The British officer moved to convert authority, at least by appearances, over Philadelphia to a civilian head, appointing Joseph Galloway as "Superintendent of the Police in the City and its Environs & Superintendent of Exports to and From Philadelphia." Galloway had attended the First Continental Congress as a delegate from Pennsylvania, where he put forward a plan for a degree of independence for the colonies that was rejected by a narrow margin. This did not sit well with the Pennsylvania delegate. His views soon caught the suspicion of more independent-minded delegates and late in 1776, Galloway fled to New York and into British safety.

British Costume, 1777.

This image shows the uniform of a British drummer during the American Revolution, from the year of 1777. (nypl)

Now back in Philadelphia, Galloway's task was to try and bring back a sense of normalcy to the city. His initiatives included encouraging any newspaper editors still in Philadelphia to continue operation and curbing inflation for foodstuffs. More importantly, for both the British and Galloway's own reputation, the Marylander tried to promote the high degree of loyalist fervor in the City of Brotherly Love.

With the opening of the Delaware River, goods and commodities began to flow into the city, but there was still hardship to endure. Prices on certain goods, such as salt, the eighteenth century substitute for refrigeration, soared to the point that Galloway enacted price controls. But this simply served to drive the selling of salt more into the black market.

In addition, people sold off household goods

TOP: Silhouette of the residence used by Howe, later the home of presidents George Washington and John Adams. (es)

RIGHT: At the front door of the executive home, the Liberty Bell Center is visible in the background. (es)

Looking in the opposite direction of the photos above, from the interior of Howe's home and headquarters of the British command during the occupation of Philadelphia. The Independence National Park visitor center is visible in the background. (es)

and loot that was confiscated by the British from around 600 abandoned homes belonging to rebel sympathizers, which showed that hard currency still ruled over paper. Another issue that arose was the scarcity of wood, as the army consumed 600 cords daily (a full cord being a stack of wood that is four feet wide, four feet high, and

An archeology display shows off part of the original foundation of the residence used by Howe. (es)

eight feet long). What was not auctioned from those homes that could be burned quickly disappeared to keep soldiers and the remaining civilians warm for the winter months.

Although Howe usually abhorred winter campaigning, he did try to bait the Continentals into action in early December. Prior to moving to Valley Forge, Washington's army was in the Whitemarsh Township encampment at Edge Hill. The proximity of the Continental army conjured up memories of the previous winter's quick forays at Trenton and then Princeton that led to disaster for the British cause. Thus, on December 4, Howe set out with the majority of the British and Hessian forces, leaving approximately 3,000 men behind to defend Philadelphia.

Washington was warned of the British advance and took the precaution of sending away his heavy baggage and striking the tents of the encampment, but he maintained his defensive position. With limited cavalry, the Continentals made the going as tough as they could for the advancing British. By December 5, Howe was within three miles of the Continental army encampment, and the campfires to their front had initially convinced the British that Washington's army was larger than originally thought. By daybreak, the trick

Sir William Howe, the British commander, captured Philadelphia in 1777 but nonetheless faced scrutiny about his campaign decisions. (nypl)

With the British occupation, the building that once saw independence declared now held as prisoners some of the men captured while trying to make that dream a reality. The British also used the structure as their main guard house and a hospital. (es)

was uncovered, but had bought Washington another night to continue preparations.

Howe did not strike and the antagonists spent the next two days maintaining their respective positions. The British commander then employed the tactic that worked so well at Brandywine, a feint on the center and a strike around the flank. Although reports on the battle are contradictory, it was evident that at this engagement the British were unable to turn the flank. Howe also refused to assault the center of the line directly, believing the venture was not worth the bloodshed.

Four more days passed before Washington broke camp and retreated across the Schuylkill River on a temporary wooden span. When the British pursued, the bridge was dismantled, eliminating the chance for Howe's forces to attack.

The effort to lure the Americans into the open for a pitched battle ended there. This was the last major attempt by the British

commander to defeat Washington's main force. Besides failing to land a knock-out blow, to add to Howe's woes that winter he would have to answer the inevitable communiques that would be coming from London and Lord George Germain, the secretary of state for America, who was responsible for overseeing the war effort and assisting Lord North, the prime minister. Howe was wearying from the war effort and would learn in late October about the disaster that befell Gen. John Burgoyne and his British force at Saratoga in upstate New York.

A view of downtown Philadelphia from the countryside, with a date of November 1777. (nypl)

This set the precedent for the British during the winter of 1777–78, moments of good fortune and military success, such as the opening of the Delaware River or the early May victory at Crooked Billet. However, there was plenty of news that soured the good fortune: the defeat of Burgoyne, the repetitiveness and boredom that accompanied any winter encampment, and in early spring the news of Prime Minister Lord North's government's more conciliatory approach toward the rebellious colonies.

When the conciliatory bills and copies of North's speech were printed and posted, the reaction among the British soldiers and officer corps was defiance to the point that North was

Elferth's Alley, Philadelphia— a city street since the first houses were built in 1720.
(es)(es)

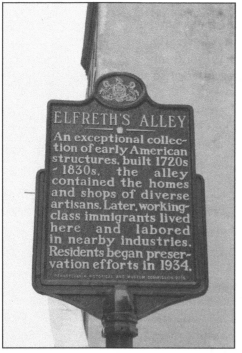

burned in effigy and many of these printed materials were publicly ripped up and trashed. A disconnect had formed, with the belief still strong in the British rank-and-file and junior officer corps that a military victory that would end the strife was still possible. Politicians back in London looked at the war through the lens of continued cost and political capital and what the new alliance between the colonies and France would do to change the dynamic of the conflict. Yet, the opposition in Parliament raised a most valid point, put into words by William Pitt: "If I were an American as I am an Englishman, while

One of the brick structures of Elferth's Alley shows the style and construction during the time of the American Revolution. (es)

a foreign troop was landed in my country I never would lay down my arms—never, never."

Captain Johann Ewald, the jaeger captain, would agree, as he found that conciliation was not popular with the citizens of Philadelphia who favored the American cause. For them, independence was the chief requirement of any conciliatory talks with the British government. The German captain recorded no surprise at this viewpoint.

With the news from London came Germain's reply on February 4, 1778, that Howe's resignation request was accepted, and that Gen. Sir Henry Clinton was named as his successor. A proper send-off for Howe was agreed upon and the date of May 18 was set. Captain John Andre, the chief planner, called it "The Misquianza." Twenty-two officers pledged 140 pounds, but the cost would grow enormously. In fact, some of the materials cost 12,000 pounds!

The Union Jack flying outside a home on Elferth Alley serves as a reminder of the Loyalist sentiment many Americans felt during the Revolution. (es)

After all the preparations were completed, the send-off began at 4:00 p.m. with over 400 guests in attendance. There was a medieval tournament and a huge reception, with fireworks, dancing and spirits to drink and toast the night away. The only hiccup was the sudden sound of sporadic gunfire, which gave everyone a momentary pause. This was due to a minor action out on the British front lines, aimed at interrupting the festivities when Capt. Allan McLane and a few Continental dragoons snuck up and were able to set fire to a few of the abatis, the wooden stakes, that guarded one of the redoubts. The minor disturbance was explained away by attributing the noise as part of the firework demonstration, and everybody went back to partying.

What the partying could not mask, though, was the feeling of uncertainty of the past campaigning year and for the year unfolding: for what had the capture of Philadelphia brought? The Continental army was still ensconced over the horizon, Burgoyne's army was marching into

Imagine the entire city with streets similar to this one— and the tramp of patrolling British soldiers on those cobblestones. (es)

captivity, and the administration at home had turned to the idea of putting out a conciliatory feeler to the rebels. For the foot soldiers manning the defenses or huddled in confiscated abandoned buildings throughout Philadelphia, the winter months dragged on, with mundane repetitiveness.

All that changed though, when an American deserter approached a picket post. His news would bring one more opportunity for Howe to argue his case of good generalship when he returned to London.

Timely and Handsome
CHAPTER TWELVE
May 20, 1778

The winter of 1777–78 had not been kind to the Marquis de Lafayette. The French aristocrat had snuck across the Atlantic Ocean in the summer of 1777, landing near Georgetown, South Carolina, in June. Making his way north, on July 31 he was made a major general by the Continental Congress with the help of Benjamin Franklin, who had recently returned from France, and vouched for the credentials of the enterprising young Frenchman.

In early August, Lafayette was a dinner guest of George Washington when the general came to the capital to confer with Congress, and the two quickly drew a liking to each other akin to a father-son relationship. Upon his arrival with the Continental army, Lafayette joined Washington's staff, endearing himself to the general by volunteering to serve without pay. He also made it clear that he had come to learn and not to teach Washington or other American generals how to conduct military operations. It was a positive change from other foreign-born aristocrats and military officers.

While serving during the battle of Brandywine on September 11, 1777, Lafayette received a painful wound to the leg but stayed on the field to

At one point during the actions around Barren Hill, Lafayette climbed the original steeple to peer at the British lines. (es)

British General James Grant led a portion of Howe's forces at the battle of Barren Hill. He famously boasted he could march from one end of America to the other with a mere 5,000 men. (nypl)

help rally retreating American soldiers. Returning to field command, he assumed leadership of a division and was active in reconnaissance missions for the remainder of the calendar year.

Yet, during the winter, he became a pawn of the political machinations of the Continental Congress and the newly created Board of War when he was asked to begin preparations for another invasion of Canada by American troops. When he arrived at the staging area of Albany, New York, he discovered a dearth of supplies and a lack of manpower, which dampened his spirits and his ardor for the mission. After informing Washington of the situation, Lafayette used his time in New York to positive effect by cultivating a relationship with the Oneida Native Americans, one of the only tribes to ally itself with the patriot cause during the American Revolution. For the young Frenchman, this connection would prove beneficial in the very near future.

With his return to the more familiar environs in Pennsylvania, Lafayette was present in the encampment when news arrived of the formal treaty with France, which was publicized in March of 1778. During the spring, word from spies and scouts alerted Washington to the impending evacuation of Philadelphia by British troops, now under a new commander, Gen. Henry Clinton, who had replaced William Howe after that general's resignation the previous October.

Washington was not about to take a chance that news of an evacuation was false; the movement detected by his scouts and spies could be preparations for an offensive against the American troops. The Virginian decided to establish a reconnaissance in force and chose Lafayette to lead the expedition. Picking Lafayette would help put the young Marquis at ease, since the winter and the aborted Canadian invasion had weighed heavily on his mind. But entrusting such a crucial mission to a young, brash, and mostly inexperienced field commander was somewhat risky, so Washington packed the command with an assortment of veterans and elite units.

Joining Lafayette would be two platoons —approximately 15 to 30 men each—from Washington's Life Guards, the unit entrusted with protecting the commanding general. Another component would be 50 selected riflemen from Col. Daniel Morgan's command. These men had taken part in the climactic battle of Saratoga and would be an asset in this type of mission. Captain Allan McLane, who had initially brought to Washington the news of the British movement in Philadelphia, and his cavalrymen would also join the force along with 47 warriors from the Oneida Native Americans. When the numbers were counted, Lafayette would command a field force of 2,200 men and five pieces of artillery.

The Marquis de Lafayette's first independent command was the movement that led to the battle of Barren Hill. (nypl)

At approximately 10:00 a.m. on Monday, May 18, 1778, Lafayette's command slipped across the Schuylkill River and arrived at Barren Hill, a promontory with steep ridges located 12 miles from the environs of Philadelphia. His orders stated that it was "unadvisable" to take any permanent position, and instead he was to observe and proceed with caution. That evening, Lafayette acted contrary to his orders, but to the Frenchman's credit decided to make his encampment on the steep ridge with the river protecting his right flank and a good thoroughfare, the Ridge Road, as a line of retreat if needed. A second road led to another of the many fords that spanned the Schuylkill, and a ruined church and cemetery offered a defensible addition to the location. The Pennsylvania militia was sent to guard another road that protected Lafayette's flank, which led to the hamlet of Whitemarsh.

Daniel Morgan commanded the riflemen who served as skirmishers. His nickname was the "Old Wagoner" from his days in the French and Indian War. (nypl)

Lafayette issued orders for Captain McLane and his cavalry to patrol the Ridge Road, which was the direct access route to Philadelphia. Colonel Morgan's riflemen and the Oneida warriors would fan out in the intervening woods surrounding the road and watch for any marauders heading toward the campsite. In an oversight,

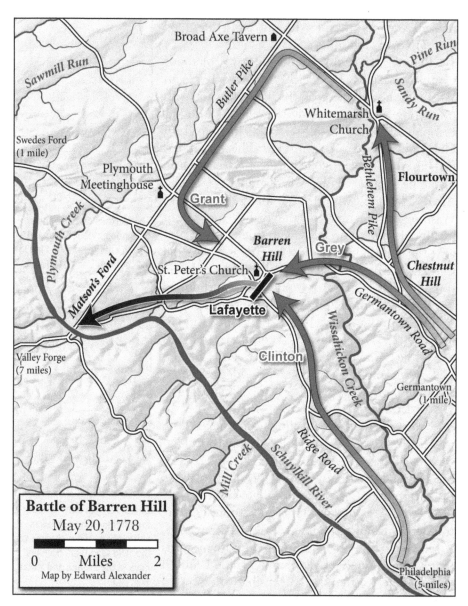

BARREN HILL MAP—A portion of the Continental army, with their Oneida Native American allies, fought the British in late May. Under the command of Gen. Marquis de Lafayette, the force showed in action that Baron von Steuben's drilling at Valley Forge during the winter encampment had made a difference for the army.

the Frenchman had assigned the 600-man detachment of the Pennsylvania militia instead of Continental army troops to guard that road to Whitemarsh, which curved around Barren Hill's steep ridges. If cut, it would put Lafayette's entire

A depiction of Oneidas in various stages of attire. Oneidas and the Tuscaroras were two of the Native American tribes that sided with the Americans during the American Revolution. This plaque honors the Oneida Native Americans who served as skirmishers and scouts during the battle of Barren Hill. Six of their warriors fell during the engagement. (nypi)

command in a dire predicament. Why the militia was assigned this role was never reported and would prove almost disastrous for the Americans.

Meanwhile, "The Misquianza" had also been planned for the night of May 18. Although command had been passed over to Clinton, Howe, still in the city for another week, would be giving orders until his departure, as precedent dictated. Lafayette may have become aware of this gala from spies that Captain McLane had led to headquarters for their reports.

Although it's hard to substantiate that Lafayette was aware of it, the relaxed atmosphere within the American encampment suggests that orders had not been passed along to maintain the utmost diligence. Exposing this condition sometime that day, a soldier from the American command had snuck away from camp and made his way toward the big city.

That soldier arrived at a British sentry post in the early morning of May 19, and his information was a goldmine for the redcoats. The deserter gave the precise location of Lafayette's forces and also confirmed that the Frenchman was in command. Furthermore, the deserter recounted for the British the approach he had taken to reach their lines: he had simply walked down the road that led to Whitemarsh and not a soul impeded his route. The Pennsylvania militia, under Gen. James Potter, was not in position and the town of

A stone marker in St. Peter's Cemetery near the spot where the Americans decamped during the expedition that resulted in the battle of Barren Hill. (es)

Whitemarsh and the road behind the American lines was unprotected.

Even in the midst of the revelry, Howe could see the golden opportunity that now presented itself. Within manageable marching distance was an American force with an unprotected flank commanded by the notable Frenchman, the Marquis de Lafayette. Capturing Lafayette and crushing this American force would be the fitting epitaph for Howe before he went home to face questions of his leadership in the conflict.

Orders quickly disseminated from British headquarters, and as Howe rode out of the city (in a carriage no less), he did so with his brother Lord Richard Howe and General Clinton as spectators. The British plan called for Gen. James Grant and 5,000 men to follow the road through Whitemarsh and gain the rear of Lafayette's position, effectively blocking the retreat route to Valley Forge. General Charles Grey with another force would close off the nearest ford, eliminating that escape route. The main force, under the personal direction of Howe, would attack up the Ridge Road and assail Lafayette from the front. It was a classic Howe maneuver—envelopment of the flanks—coupled this time with a frontal assault to break the Americans' will.

With the longer approaches, Grant's and Grey's forces were on the road that evening. Howe's force left later. Much of the British garrison of Philadelphia was on this endeavor with the intention of destroying Lafayette and his command.

According to one report, as Grant's men advanced through the town of Whitemarsh, the tramp and clanging of accoutrements woke up a sleeping Pennsylvania militia officer. This soldier quickly sized up the force making its way down the thoroughfare, and, without taking time to dress, slipped off in his night garments to awaken Lafayette. After moving to the point of exhaustion, luck was on the side of the Pennsylvanian, who happened to stumble upon a surgeon of the American army, who relayed the news to the general.

Although skeptical at first, since he supposed militia guarded the road (which they did not), Lafayette did send out an aide to ascertain this bit of intelligence. The aide quickly returned confirming that the British were advancing and that they had almost gained the rear of the American position.

Digesting the aide's report, Lafayette's thinking was interrupted by the sudden outburst of musketry. In advance of the American position were the Oneidas and Col. Morgan's riflemen. Deployed as skirmishers, whose task was to

Lafayette encamped here in his first independent command. It was a major responsibility for the young Frenchmen because of the untested nature of the army after its long, trying winter. (psg)

From the graveyard of St. Peter's Church, Lafayette organized the defense of American forces during the battle of Barren Hill—and then their retreat afterward. (es)

provide warning of any approach, these men had detected the British advance—the portion under Howe's personal command—and the firefight had begun. With the fire intensifying, Capt. Allan McLane came to report its source to Lafayette.

To the young Frenchman's credit he quickly understood the British intentions and acted decisively. He knew he had to gather his forces and beat a hasty retreat toward the river. Meanwhile, on the skirmish line, the Oneidas and Morgan's riflemen had slowed the British advance. Yet, the disparity in numbers between the main British force and the pickets became noticeable, and hoping to brush aside this minor hindrance, Howe ordered a cavalry charge.

With the thundering of hooves bearing down on them, the Oneidas unleashed their own secret weapon, their traditional war whoop, and continued the melee. This tactic unnerved the British horse soldiers, frightening both man and beast, who had never heard the blood-curdling sound. The Oneida battle cry created a few moments of near panic in the ranks of the British cavalry and scattered them. This delayed the advance of the British infantry, as a few moments were needed to reorganize and order the foot soldiers forward.

Lafayette's forces continued to pull back.

In another daring tactic, the Frenchman had ordered a contingent of men and two artillery pieces to block Grant's advance and to act aggressively, giving the impression that they were larger in number than they really were. Here the young nobleman correctly sized up Grant's cautious nature. Grant was convinced that the woods were filled with enemy soldiers arriving on the scene, and he could not be persuaded otherwise. He changed direction away from the ford where he was initially headed, which would have blocked Lafayette's escape. Instead he moved to the church residing on Barren Hill, where he believed the enemy force was still positioned. But instead of finding the enemy, Grant's advance brought him into contact with Howe's forces coming up the other side of the heights.

The stone wall of the Lutheran Church was used for Lafayette's defensive stand before his retreat to Matson's Ford. (es)

As Lafayette and his men escaped across Matson's Ford, lookouts from Mount Joy in Valley Forge had given warning, and signal guns started organizing the various brigades to the action unfolding down the road. The British could also hear the sound of the guns and knew that the chance to bag Lafayette and his force had evaporated. Reinforcements could be headed their way, so Howe prudently called in his scattered commands and issued orders to begin the retrograde movement back to Philadelphia.

The last action of the day took place near the Schuylkill River as the Oneidas and Morgan's riflemen skirmished with British dragoons, or horse soldiers. A few of the rearguard were captured as they made their way toward the water and British dragoons kept up the fire until the Oneidas and Morgan's men gained the opposite bank, where their return fire finally convinced these last British soldiers to depart as well.

Although largely forgotten in the history of the American Revolution, the Oneidas played an important role in the battle of Barren Hill, suffering a few casualties and being the last organized body to retreat across the Schuylkill River. But their commitment and courage under fire, not just at Barren Hill, but especially in the northern theater, would not go completely unrecognized. With George Washington's encouragement, a few of the Oneidas and Tuscaroras, another of the Native American tribes that fought on the American side, would be commissioned as officers in accordance with their bravery and acumen in battle.

Oneida Native Americans served as skirmishers and scouts, and six of them gave their lives at the battle of Barren Hill. (es)

In the meantime, however, one aspect of the affair at Barren Hill had been born out under the duress of a retreat and enemy fire. For the past several weeks the men of the Continental army had been under intense training by Baron von Steuben, but no real action had unfolded. Barren Hill was the first chance to prove whether the Baron's training had taken hold.

When the retreat was ordered, the American forces moved off in a structured and compact body, not the Native American style that had dominated their retreats in prior engagements. In moving swiftly into column from battle line, Lafayette's forces were able to make it to the ford and escape to safety in the shortest amount of time. Although Lafayette and his men were surprised by the British advance, their coolness under fire, adherence to commands from general and line officers, and their retreat showed they had learned well what had been taught on the training ground.

This picture captures the view from the front line of the American forces on May 20, 1778. The road leading down off the hill was the route used by the British advance. Lafayette organized his defense and masterly retreat from the churchyard, which is off to the left of this photograph. (psg)

In defeat, a valuable lesson had been unknowingly passed, and from that, the future looked a little brighter for the Continental army.

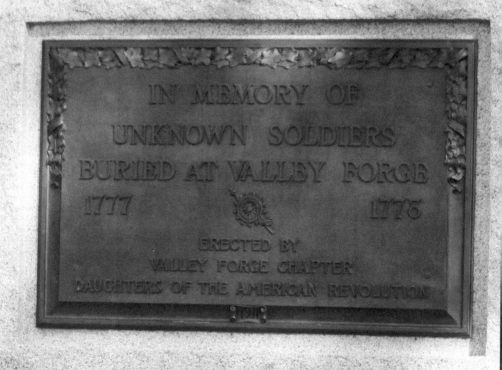

Conclusion
June 19, 1778–onwards

Six months to the day. One-hundred eighty-two days. On June 19, 1778, the Continental army, revitalized, reinforced, and re-trained, marched out of Valley Forge. Numbering over 15,000 men, the winter had forged them into a credible military force.

That May, with the knowledge of the Franco-American alliance, Gen. Sir Henry Clinton, the new British general-in-chief in America, had begun preparing for the evacuation of Philadelphia. News began leaking out of the city through refugees and the spy and scout network that Washington had established in the previous six months. By June 17, Philadelphia saw the last of the British occupying force leave the wharves along the Delaware River as the navy evacuated loyalists and the usual heavy equipment that accompanies any army in the field. The British army had by that date crossed the river and started its trek across New Jersey toward New York City.

As May became June, with this news quickly approaching the Potts's house and Washington's desk, the general prudently called a council of war with his top officers. He laid before them various courses that the army could take in response to

By the time the army marched away in June 1778, more than 2,500 soldiers had perished at Valley Forge. The majority of their names are lost to history, but their memory is honored by a monument at the encampment site. (psg)

As the soldiers huddle around the small fire trying to keep warm, Washington looks over a map, planning the next campaign and hoping the sacrifice of his men during that winter will lead to victory in the coming year. (nypl)

the British leaving Philadelphia. General Charles Lee, the second-in-charge of the Continental army who had returned during the winter encampment from his captivity, was adamant the enemy would retrace their steps to the Chesapeake Bay. Washington responded by reading from the reports of the activity around New York City, chiefly, an increase in small watercraft activity gathering and staging in locations that would allow them to easily transport Clinton's ground forces back to that metropolis.

With Lee assuaged, Washington posed a few questions to the council to consider: Should the army follow Clinton on parallel routes across New Jersey and rendezvous with the expected French fleet around New York City? The combined

Charles Lee was one of the most experienced military officers in the Continental Army. He was Washington's second in command until his capture by the British on December 12, 1776. He was exchanged and returned to duty during the winter encampment at Valley Forge. (nypl)

Franco-American army and navy could either assault or besiege the British. Or, should the army quickly decamp and strike a blow at the rearguard of the British column, further boosting the morale of the troops of the Continental army while equally eroding British morale both in America and back in Great Britain? Lastly, should Washington and his generals decide on a place to entice the British into one climatic battle, using the entire Continental army and militia forces available with the intention of crushing the British army to swiftly end the conflict?

These three options were then discussed by the gathering of generals. The last, precipitating a major conflict, was quickly overruled. The evacuation of Philadelphia, seen as the capital of the fledgling United States, was a victory, and it would be unwise to hazard that by risking a major defeat early in the campaigning season.

Sir Henry Clinton assumed command of the British army in North America upon Howe's resignation. (nypl)

Lee continued to speak out against any offensive action that would provoke the enemy, still believing in the superiority of the British army and the inability of the Continental army to win a battle against them. Another officer, Gen. Benedict Arnold, believed a small rearguard action would escalate into a larger-scale engagement that the Americans may struggle to win.

Washington listened to the points, reasons, and arguments of his generals but did not present his viewpoint. Instead, he remained stoic and impassive throughout. At the very end, he finally gave his opinion, the one that the Continental army would follow.

The army would march from Valley Forge and track the British through New Jersey, staying close enough to take advantage of any opportunity that might arise.

Winter is typically a transitioning period in the calendar, laying the foundation for spring where life is renewed in the natural world. The winter of 1777–78 was the same for the Continental army at Valley Forge. The bedraggled, variously trained, low-provisioned force that tramped up the Gulph Road on that past December left their winter cantonment six months later a completely different force, a transition not only for the army, but also for the men themselves, and the cause for which they would continue to fight.

When taking stock of what had transpired during that short period of time, the changes are even more remarkable, starting with the general-in-chief. Washington had solidified his hold on the Continental army, warded off potential detractors and potential usurpers within a cadre of dissatisfied generals, and survived political pressure from both the Continental Congress and the Pennsylvania legislature. At the conclusion of the Valley Forge encampment, Washington had also built a steady bloc of more friendly politicians, including the current president of the Continental Congress, Henry Laurens. One could argue that Washington had given an insight into his future

political mindset and approach during those six months. He also grew in stature in the eyes of the men under his command by championing their cause, sharing, within reason, their hardships by selecting winter quarters within Valley Forge, and by making the decisions that would secure their well-being and improve their trade with changes to the quartermaster department and inspector general position.

A Frenchman left this lasting impression when he first cast a gaze on the Virginian:

> *I cannot describe the impression that the first sight of that great man made upon me. I could not keep my eyes from that imposing countenance; grave yet not severe; affable without familiarity. Its predominant expression was calm dignity, through which you could trace the strong feelings of the patriot and discern the father as well as the commander of his soldiers.*

Although subsistence would remain at critical levels throughout the army's stay at Valley Forge, installing Nathanael Greene as quartermaster general would pay dividends before the next campaigning season as supplies were stockpiled in depots along potential routes of march,

The writing on the archway sums up the importance of this encampment toward the war effort and what it stood for regarding the Continental army and their continued existence. (psg)

fraud and waste were investigated, and better communication, orders, and book-keeping averted problems and allowed supplies to be attained more quickly. Unfortunately, as historian Willard M. Wallace wrote, the "suffering was due to American mismanagement, graft, speculation, and indifference, more than to the enemy or the weather," as one can infer from the rich harvest of Pennsylvania crops being sold to the British instead of to the Americans. By encampment's end, one out of every four soldiers perished, numbers that weighed heavily on the minds of Washington and his new quartermaster general. Greene strove hard to combat this but was faced with a near-impossible task. That he made any headway at all showed his indispensability to the position with which he was tasked.

In the ensuing years, Greene would be the subject of investigations into his actions as quartermaster general, each failing to uncover any illegal dealings or fraud or waste, and showing without a doubt that Washington had selected the right man for the job in the winter that won the war. The Rhode Islander eventually returned to active field command in the Southern theater.

His eccentricities and multi-lingual grasp of obscenities aside, Baron Frederich Wilhelm von Steuben was second in importance only to Washington that winter. His ability to train the army in tactics and military maneuvers, ranging from the individual to brigade level, was truly remarkable. He adapted techniques and teachings from the old-world militaries and made them fit the psyche and military acumen of the American soldier. The quick action at Barren Hill in May provided a glimpse into this newly trained American army and built hope for that same presence on the battlefield when the entire army marched out of Valley Forge.

Even the rank-and-file had gone through a transformation, as longer enlistments, new recruits, and better camp practices all became refined during the Valley Forge experience. The men who survived would be forever changed. With improved morale, better training, and access to better foodstuffs on the immediate horizon, the men's suffering seemed, for the moment, behind them as spring unfolded in Pennsylvania and the active campaigning season erupted again.

On June 19, more than 15,000 men in 80 infantry regiments, 12 companies of artillery, and accompanying cavalry swung into line and proceeded to the northeast. The gazes of the men were toward New Jersey and the future, where potential success could lead to the attainment of American independence. If William T. Trego had painted the exodus of Valley Forge, this image would have shown a different line of march and different words to explain what the viewer was casting his or her gaze upon. Words such as . . .

Relief.

Hopefulness.

Expectation.

Prowess.

Valley Forge truly forged the American army and was the winter that won the war.

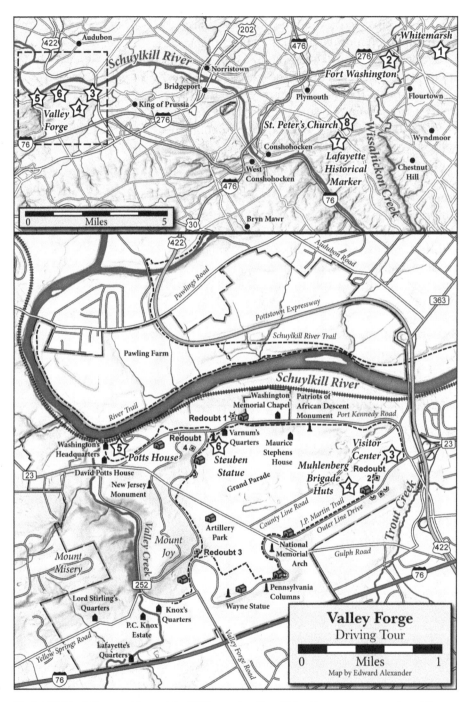

Driving Tour—A three-part tour of the Whitemarsh action, Valley Forge encampment, and Barren Hill battlefield.

Touring the Battlefield

→ ## TO STOP 1

You may wish to start the driving tour at Valley Forge National Historical Park, but to follow the route of the army, the driving tour begins at Whitemarsh, where the Continental army began their last march of 1777.

GPS: 40° 7' 26.79 N, 75° 11' 33.65 W

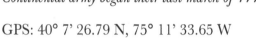

Stop 1 – Whitemarsh

In this area, the Continental army encamped from November 2 until December 11, when they marched toward their permanent winter encampment at Valley Forge. The Emlen house served as the headquarters of George Washington during this time. George Emlen III built the house but passed away in 1776. The house was razed in 2014. A Pennsylvania Historical and Museum Commission sign now marks the general location.

➡ TO STOP 2

Head northwest on Pennsylvania Avenue and in less than one-tenth of a mile turn left onto Camp Hill Road. Follow Camp Hill Road for approximately one and a half miles and then turn right onto South Bethlehem Pike. In approximately six-tenths of a mile the stone marker will be on your right at the entrance to the William Boulton Dixon American Legion Post (493 South Bethlehem Pike, Fort Washington, Pennsylvania).

GPS: 40° 7' 52.55 N, 75° 12' 55.39 W

Stop 2 - Fort Washington Stone Monument

As the marker depicts, the redoubt that the Americans employed during the battle of Whitemarsh, fought between December 5–8, 1777, was 700 yards to the south. After Howe refused to seriously assault the defensive works constructed by the Americans, Washington pulled the army out of these lines. This resulted in the last engagement of 1777. All that awaited the Americans now was to find a place to winter.

➡ TO STOP 3

You will proceed from the monument to Valley Forge National Historical Park. The quickest route would be to follow signs to the Pennsylvania Turnpike (I-276). To do so, make a right out of the parking lot of the American Legion and then make a right onto Pennsylvania Avenue in approximately six-tenths of a mile. For about another six-tenths of a mile, stay on Pennsylvania Avenue until you see signs for the turnpike. You will go on I-276/Pennsylvania Turnpike West to Valley Forge National Historical Park.

This is a toll road, however, but is the quickest route. In approximately 13 miles you will see the exit for Valley Forge (Exit 326).
To avoid the toll road, there are a few options, but best to consult a navigational device if proceeding with this choice.

Address to Valley Forge National Historical Park:
1400 North Outer Line Dr., King of Prussia, PA 19406
GPS: 40 ° 6'4.993 N by 75 ° 25'20.203 W

* This driving tour details the most important locations at Valley Forge National Historical Park. A more detailed driving tour is available upon request from The Encampment Store inside the park visitor center. The entire driving tour for the national historical park is 10 miles. *

Stop 3–Valley Forge Visitor Center

In 1893, Valley Forge was preserved as Pennsylvania's first state park. In 1976, for the Bicentennial, the commonwealth gifted the property to the United States. On July 4 of that year, President Gerald Ford signed legislation that created Valley Forge National Historical Park. Today, the park covers 3,500 acres and has more than 26 miles of hiking trails.

Opened to the public in spring 2020, a new visitor center at Valley Forge replaces the original 1976 building (pictured below). The new VC has an encampment shop bookstore, exhibits, park film, information desk, and restrooms. More than 300 museum objects are featured throughout the new five-part exhibit area, which immerses the public in the six-month long encampment. From this stop you can start the tour, which will coincide in part with the driving tour designed by the National Park Service.

(psg)

⟶ TO STOP 4

After leaving the visitor center, follow the signs for the "Encampment Tour Stop." The next stop will be the Muhlenberg Brigade Huts.

GPS: 40° 5' 50.02 N, 75° 25' 33.42 W

Stop 4—Muhlenberg Brigade Huts

(psg)

(psg)

After parking on the left (south) side of North Outer Line Drive, you will see the huts to the north side of the road. Although reconstructed, these nine huts provide a glimpse into what the permanent shelters for the Continental army would have resembled during the winter encampment. During certain times of the year, living history is conducted here to show the life of a soldier during the Valley Forge winter.

John Peter Gabriel Muhlenberg, a native Pennsylvanian, was an ordained priest in the Anglican Church, but served a Lutheran congregation in Virginia. He was very active in Virginia patriotic movements, leading the Committee of Safety and Correspondence for the local county. He also secured election to the House of Burgesses in 1774, along with being a delegate to the first Virginia Convention. He was granted permission to raise the 8th Virginia Regiment for the burgeoning Continental army, becoming the unit's first colonel.

By the time of Valley Forge, Muhlenberg had been promoted to brigadier general in the Virginia Line and commanded the brigade, a part of Nathanael Greene's division, during the encampment.

➤ TO STOP 5

As you drive the tour road, you will pass on your left-hand side the National Memorial Arch. Feel free to stop at this tour stop (Valley Forge National Historical Park Encampment Tour Stop #3). Funds were appropriated in 1911 by the United States Congress, construction began in 1914, and the dedication ceremonies were conducted on June 19, 1917.

As you proceed on the tour road, there will be numerous monuments along the way. The next stop will be Encampment Tour Stop #5 which is Washington's headquarters.

GPS: 40° 6' 6.39 N,
75° 27' 40.26 W

Stop 5 – Potts's House

As you proceed down the hill from the parking lot you will see the stone structure of the Potts house ahead of you. From this vantage point you are starting at the nerve center of the Continental army and the military heartbeat of the American Revolution. When the structure is open you can tour the rooms of the building. If your visit coincides with a time the historical structure is closed, a virtual tour is available via YouTube.

As you make your way along the winding path to the Potts's house and outbuildings, a collection of reconstructed huts is to your left. These replicas housed the "Life Guards" for George Washington. This unit traced its organization back to a March 11, 1776 general order while the army was encamped at Cambridge, Massachusetts.

His Excellency depends upon the Colonels for good Men, such as they can recommend for their sobriety, honesty and good behavior; he wishes them to be from five feet eight Inches high, to five feet ten Inches; handsomely and well made, and as there is nothing in his eyes more desirable than Cleanliness in a Soldier, he desires that particular attention be made in the choice of such men as are clean and spruce.

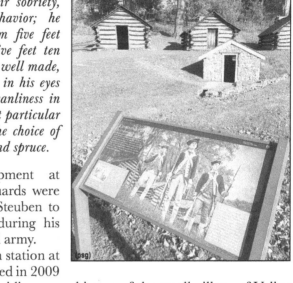

During the encampment at Valley Forge, the Life Guards were the unit selected by von Steuben to be the model company during his training of the Continental army.

Built in 1911, the train station at Valley Forge was refurbished in 2009 and is now a museum providing more history of the small village of Valley Forge and Washington's headquarters.

➤ TO STOP 6

Turn left after leaving the parking lot of Washington's headquarters. Proceed straight instead of turning right up the hillside. The next stop will be Encampment Tour Stop #8 at the von Steuben Statue.

GPS: 40° 6' 11.34 N, 75° 26' 50.96 W

Stop 6—Baron von Steuben Statue

A bronze statue, simply known as the von Steuben Monument, gazes eternally over the Grand Parade field, where the Baron spent countless hours during the winter of 1778. The statue, created by sculptor J. Otto Schweizer, stands on a six foot eight inch pedestal with the general measuring in at eight and a half feet on top.

The Valley Forge statue of

the Baron is an exact replica of the general in Utica, New York. But, showing the continued importance of what von Steuben did at Valley Forge, the difference between the two is a plaque that depicts a scene of drilling during that winter that won the war. When you stand beside the general, you are gazing out into the fields where the Continental army went through their transformation. This field may be one of the most crucial spots during the entire American Revolutionary War.

Imagine seeing companies of men going through various paces, onlookers gawking at the fence line, and the Baron, ever present, yelling out commands and asking his aide to translate when the troops needed to be cursed at

⟶ TO STOP 7

After leaving the parking lot for the Baron von Steuben Statue, you will pass on your left the Memorial Chapel. Feel free to stop and tour this structure and grounds.

A sermon by Reverend Doctor W. Herbert Burk inspired the construction of the church, which stands as both a memorial to George Washington and

(psg)

the Continental army and also is an active Episcopal parish. The cornerstones were laid on June 19, 1903, the 125th anniversary of the march out of Valley Forge. According to the history, the money was raised by small donations, "nickels and dimes," with the exterior of the structure completed in 1917 and the interior finished four years later. A later addition was the bell

(nhp)

tower, standing at 102 feet, and built with money raised and donated by the Daughters of the American Revolution. World War II interrupted the construction, which had started in 1941, but the project was completed by the end of the decade and dedicated in 1953. There is an exact replica of the Liberty Bell on display in the tower.

The next stop will be the two sites attributed to the battle of Barren Hill.

Proceed out of Valley Forge National Historical Park, turn right at the light onto North Gulph Road, and in one and a half miles merge onto I-76 East toward Philadelphia. Take Exit 331B onto I-476 toward Plymouth Meeting. Keep left to merge onto I-476 North. In approximately two and four-tenths miles take Exit 18A toward Conshohocken. In approximately three and a half miles, the blue historical sign will be on your left, in front of the Masonic Village of Lafayette Hill complex.

Barren Hill Driving Tour Stops

The area around the battlefield has been completely obscured by modern growth and development. Please take caution while traversing the few stops that comprise the Barren Hill Driving Tour.

GPS: 40° 4' 42.83 N, 75° 14' 53.34 W

Stop 7—Lafayette Historical Marker

The Pennsylvania Historical Marker is located where the Marquis de Lafayette encamped his 2,000-man force the night of May 19, 1778. This would be Lafayette's first independent command and as the sign reads, after Howe's withdrawal, the Frenchman would show the pluck of his audacious nature by reoccupying the heights. The area today is also known as Lafayette Hill.

➔ TO STOP 8

Turn right out of the parking lot for the Masonic Village and proceed approximately four-tenths of a mile, then turn right onto Church Road. In about another tenth of a mile the church will be on your left. Parking will be in a lot on the right.

GPS: 40° 5' 3.87 N, 75° 14' 58.44 W

(psg)

Stop 8—St. Peter's Church

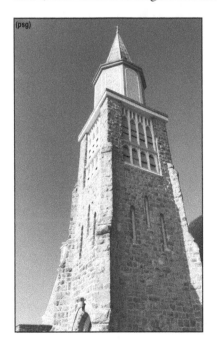

(psg)

From the steeple of the original church, Lafayette quickly and confidently directed his command, organizing the retreat to Matson's Ford. The men under his leadership showed the extent of training that von Steuben had imparted. Within the cemetery rests a stone marker where the men under Lafayette encamped and also the combined grave of six Oneida Native Americans who gave their lives to the cause.

From the original steeple, Lafayette observed some of the action that May day.

This ends the driving tour, but other historic sites, including Germantown, Philadelphia, Brandywine Battlefield, and Paoli, among others, are readily accessible and a short drive from Barren Hill.

SACRED TO THE MEMORY OF

HUGH MERCER,

BRIGADIER - GENERAL
IN THE ARMY OF
THE UNITED STATES.

HE DIED ON THE 12th OF JANUARY, 1777,
OF THE WOUNDS HE RECEIVED
ON THE 3d OF THE SAME MONTH,
NEAR PRINCETOWN, IN NEW JERSEY,
BRAVELY DEFENDING THE
LIBERTIES OF AMERICA.

THE CONGRESS OF THE UNITED STATES
IN TESTIMONY OF HIS VIRTUES,
AND THEIR GRATITUDE,
HAVE CAUSED THIS MONUMENT TO BE ERECTED.

To the Last Extremity
Defense of the Delaware River

APPENDIX A
BY PHILLIP S. GREENWALT

Sir William Howe's British and Hessian forces had taken the colonial capital of Philadelphia on September 26, 1777, marching in by land. But the British general still had to contend with two pesky forts on opposite banks of the Delaware River that kept the city of Philadelphia from being fully supplied for the upcoming winter. For this, cooperation between the Howe brothers—Richard Howe was the admiral in charge of the British Navy—would be essential. For six weeks the American forces in these two earthen fortifications would prove obstinate.

Fort Mercer, named for the fallen American general Hugh Mercer, who succumbed to wounds he received on January 12, 1777, at the Battle of Princeton, was constructed on the 400-acre plantation of James and Ann Whitail beginning in April of that year. Ignoring the objections of the plantation owner, who was a Quaker and thus a pacifist, the soldiers quickly dug into the dirt and sod, constructing the earthen works and then using the excavated dirt to build the parapets. This work was overseen by Thaddeus Kosciuszko, a Polish engineer who the previous year had overseen the establishment of Fort Billingsport, approximately 10 miles downriver from Fort Mercer. When completed, the fort was approximately 350 yards long and nearly 100 yards wide and had an armament of 14 cannons and room for a garrison of 1,500. Yet only 250 were present during the action in the fall of 1777.

Across the Delaware River sat the third of the three installations tasked with repelling the British from using the waterway to enter Philadelphia. Situated on Mud Island, a speck of land near the mouth of the Schuylkill River, Fort Mifflin was named for the Pennsylvania revolutionary Thomas

A statue of Hugh Mercer, sculpted by Edward Valentine, and erected in 1906, stands in Mercer's home town of Fredericksburg, Virginia. (tr)

Mifflin. Construction on the fort was actually started in 1771 by Captain John Montresor, a British engineer and cartographer who had a long service in North America. In that year, Gen.

BRIGADIER GENERAL
HUGH MERCER

Soldier. Patriot. Physician. This monument, erected by the St. Andrew's Society in 1970, honors Hugh Mercer, the Scotsman, who fell at the battle of Princeton. The fort was named in his honor in the spring of 1777. (es)

Thomas Gage, commander in chief of Great Britain's military in North America, was asked by the royal governor of Pennsylvania, John Penn, to dispatch someone to the city who could capably design defenses. The initial goal of a fortification at this location was to monitor maritime traffic entering and exiting the growing port.

Montresor would develop six potential plans for Penn and the Board of Commissioners, the group established to decide on the plan to pursue. However, all six were vetoed as being too expensive for the colony to stomach. The British engineer had proposed a price tag of £40,000. Instead the Pennsylvania Assembly passed a bill authorizing only £15,000 to purchase the island, which at the time was owned by Joseph Galloway, and materials for the actual construction.

In June of 1772, Montresor, frustrated by the lack of support for the project, returned to New York. Work continued in a dilatory nature for the next year with only the south and eastern walls being completed in stone. That was the condition of the fort until 1776 when Benjamin Franklin, in charge of a committee tasked with providing options for the defense of Philadelphia, argued for the completion of the military installation on Mud Island. Within the year, workers had completed the two remaining walls.

Along with Fort Billingsport downstream, these two forts, one made of earth and the other stone, would be the impediments to the British resupplying and making permanent their occupation of Philadelphia—the forts had to fall. The defenders were tasked with holding on "to the last extremity." One side had to win, the other had to lose. Before winter set in more fighting, dying, and destruction would unfold on the banks of the Delaware River.

Besides subduing the forts, the British had to worry about obstructions in the river itself: the Americans had employed chevaux de frise. Although used on land in Europe as anti-cavalry defenses, an underwater equivalent was designed by Robert Erskine, a Scottish immigrant who arrived in North America in 1771. For his work during the battles around New York earlier in the war, Erskine earned the appointment to Geographer and Surveyor General of the Continental Army and the rank of colonel. His modifications to the landed versions called for wooden-framed boxes measuring approximately 30 feet square made of timber and pine planks. On the end of two or three of the large timbers

The Polish émigré, Thaddeus Kosciuszko, utilized his engineering skills on the fortifications guarding the Delaware River. Besides Fort Mercer, he also helped with Fort Billingsport the previous year, and would continue to aid the American cause in both the northern and southern theaters of the war. (es)

Colonel Christopher Greene, commander of Fort Mercer, hailed from Rhode Island and was the third cousin of Maj. General Nathanael Greene. He would be killed in action at the battle of Pine's Bridge on May 14, 1781. (nypl)

Captain John Montresor was born in the British bastion of Gibraltar, on the tip of Spain, in 1736 and first came to the colonies in 1754. In late 1775, he earned the appointment of chief engineer with the rank of captain and was serving in that capacity during the attacks on the Delaware River forts in the autumn of 1777. In March 1779, he resigned his commission and returned to England. (nypl)

were iron tipped spikes. The entire device would be set under water facing downstream at an oblique angle. A chain would link the various boxes together to create a formidable barrier. Pre-determined gaps in the chain would allow for the continued passage of friendly vessels, but an unsuspecting enemy ship could have its hull gutted by those spiked ends.

Plans were quickly completed by the British to subdue the forts. On October 2, 1777, the small garrison at Fort Billingsport, 112 men under the command of Col. William Bradford, spiked the artillery, burned the barracks, and retreated. The British would destroy what remained of the fort, cut passage through two lines of chevaux de frise, and proceed toward the twin forts of Mercer and Mifflin.

Inside Fort Mercer were the 600 men under the overall command of Col. Christopher Greene, a Rhode Islander like his more well-known distant relation, Gen. Nathanael Greene. The 40-year-old officer commanded the 1st Rhode Island Regiment. Also inside the earthen walls was the 2nd Rhode Island Regiment, under the command of Col. Israel Angell.

Although Greene, who had arrived with his men on October 11, was the commander, Washington ordered Capt. Thomas Antoine Chevalier du Plessis-Mauduit to head to Fort Mifflin and "take immediate direction of the Artillery for your garrison." Plessis-Mauduit had shown his bravery during the Battle of Germantown when, according to fellow Frenchman, Marquis de Lafayette, he "was one of the two glorious, heroic young men who attacked the stone house," meaning Cliveden. The 24-year Plessis-Mauduit briefly entered the stone structure and lived to tell the tale! He would serve as field engineer as well.

The Frenchman spent the remaining time afforded him before the British onslaught to make what improvements he could. With the small size of the garrison, Plessis-Mauduit instructed a redoubt be established by essentially making an intersection within the fort and thus "transformed them [the fortifications] into a sort or large redoubt of pentagonal shape." Thus, when the British did approach, greeting them would be "a good earthen rampart with pointed stakes projecting from below the parapet, a ditch, and an abatis in front of the ditch." In this redoubt would be the 14 cannons and a garrison of between 200 and 300 men. These preparations were made knowing that the British would be arriving any day.

Across the river, Fort Mifflin, under the command of Lieut. Col. Samuel Smith, also braced for the coming enemy. One of the features that stood out to both sides was the flag pole made from a ship's mast that graced Fort Mifflin. The flag blowing in the October breeze had been made by Mrs. Elizabeth Griscom Ross, better known in history as "Betsy Ross." Betsy Ross began making flags for the Pennsylvania State Navy in May 1777.

The Americans were not the only side constructing fortifications that autumn. Captain Montresor, who as stated earlier had been ordered to design and construct Fort Mifflin prior to the war, had been overseeing defensive works around Philadelphia. He was also ordered to place and oversee the construction of batteries on Province Island, which sat opposite Fort Mifflin, although the pace seemed to Howe to be lethargic. This caused the overworked and exhausted engineer to complain in his diary, but the work progressed.

On October 11, the bombardment of Fort Mifflin began as the British had also begun to lay siege to the approaches to the island. The artillery fire at this point was more of a nuisance, but it provided the cover needed to operate against the other work, Fort Mercer. The British decided to strike Fort Mercer as it was not on an island and under the premise that the fall of one fort would necessitate the evacuation of the other, similar to what had happened in New York with the fall of

Fort Mifflin is a designated national historic landmark. The plaque explains, in part, that "this site possesses exceptional value in commemorating...the history of the United States"—the most succinct way to sum up the importance of this fort and the sacrifices made within its walls by American soldiers on the road to independence. (es)

Fort Washington and the subsequent evacuation of Fort Lee across the river.

To strike at Fort Mercer, Howe selected a force of approximately 2,000 men, all German mercenaries, under the command of Col. Carl von Donop. The men were part of Hessian and Anspach Jaegers under Col. Ludwig von Wurmb, von Donop's grenadier companies, comprising the most formidable men in the particular regiment, and the von Mirbach regiment. Accompanying the infantry was a Hessian artillery battalion consisting of ten three-pounder field pieces. These men were ferried across to Camden, New Jersey, approximately four miles north from Fort Mercer. For Colonel Donop, the shame of Trenton still hung on his shoulders, and he had volunteered for the mission to subdue Fort Mercer.

Although he had volunteered for the command, there was a grave lack of planning, as related in the account by Colonel von Wurmb about a conversation with the Hessian commander prior to embarking. Colonel Donop, when asked by Colonel von Wurmb "what instructions he had," the colonel's reply was "none" and "he was told to improvise." Not the type of answer one would wish to hear before an attack on an enemy fortification.

With the infantry would be five British Navy

ships that had sailed up from Billingsport on October 20 and had taken station outside Fort Mifflin. Their mission was to subdue that fort and then assist with the land forces in overwhelming Fort Mercer. In total, the five vessels bore 184 artillery pieces.

A mile out from the landing, New Jersey militia began skirmishing with the jaegers, and a desultory firing would continue for the majority of the march toward the fort. That night, October 21, the Germans camped at Haddonfield, but word soon emanated from the town to the garrison at Fort Mercer of the approach of an enemy force. The next day, October 22, what history would know as the Battle of Red Bank would unfold.

As the Germans approached during the morning hours, the 2nd Rhode Island, which had been sent over to Fort Mifflin, returned and brought the total number of defenders up to 500. The stage was now set for the combatants, but first a parley was beaten by drum, one of the customary procedures in 18th century warfare. Before an assault on a fortified position the defenders would be given the option to surrender, usually with honors, to avoid the potential for no quarter being given if an assault was made.

During the British bombardment, Continental soldiers took refuge from the deluge of shot and shell in the passages of Fort Mifflin. (es)

The British officer spoke loudly enough for the garrison to hear the following: "The King of England orders his rebellious subjects to lay down their arms, and they are warned that if they stand battle, no quarter will be given."

The response by the American officers, as communicated to them by Colonel Greene, comes to us from the pen of Chaplain David of the 2nd Rhode Island, "that He [Colonel

A few British artillery pieces are aimed at Fort Mifflin, showing visitors today the firepower that the American defenders had to withstand. (es)

Greene] would defend the Fort as long as he had a Man, & as to Mercy it was neither sought nor expected at their hands."

"A resolute, loud 'By God, no!'" is how the diarist Capt. Johann Ewald recorded the unofficial American answer to the parley. With the response confirmed, both sides prepared for the fighting. On the edge of the woods to which the Germans had marched, the artillery and jaeger marksmen had taken positions, and infantry formed in their attacking columns. Inside the fort, Colonel Greene signaled for the Pennsylvania Navy to lend whatever support they could.

The attack would come in three columns, with the leftmost one having to contend with the abatis. The absence of pioneers, who usually accompanied attacks wielding axes to remove the wooden stakes, meant that the infantry would have to break them down or find a way through them. This would stall this portion of the attack and subject the advance to an extended period under musketry.

Colonel Donop then addressed his officers, and following the example of their commander, they all dismounted, unsheathed their swords, and took their forward positions. The attack commenced. Colonel Greene also instilled such last-minute advice to his defenders: "Fire low, my men. They have a broad belt just above the hips. That is where you must aim."

The abatis did hold up a column of grenadiers attacking the southern portions, unable to scale the nine-foot section of the walls because they did not bring scaling ladders on this expedition. One column was able to scale the northern ramparts, which had been evacuated by the Americans. However, these attackers were stopped with enfilading fire when trying to get through another set of abatis outside the main wall of the fort. Casualties continued to mount. Even the British Navy suffered, as two of the five vessels ran aground trying to engage the pesky smaller ships of the Pennsylvania Navy and attempting to avoid the cheveaux de frise strung across the Delaware River.

Lieutenant Colonel Samuel Smith was commander of Fort Mifflin until he was wounded on November 11. He recovered to fight at the battle of Monmouth Court House. He would don his uniform again during the War of 1812 and defend another post, Baltimore, during the British invasion in September 1814. (nypl)

One of the casualties was Colonel Donop himself, mortally wounded with a musket ball through the thigh. Two other German colonels would also fall during the assault on Fort Mercer. Although the Hessians were able to reach the gate of the fort and a few intrepid attackers mounted the palisades, they could not breach the walls and suffered tremendously.

After 40 minutes, the attack had reached its zenith, and the Hessians began to pull back. The nine-foot walls proved impregnable to attackers not suppled with the tools needed to fight against a fortification. The men trickled back 400 yards to their artillery line, where the attack started. Eventually the retreat would continue back to Haddonfield.

In the field, ditches, and trenches lay dead and wounded Germans. The official Hessian casualty report listed 371 killed, wounded, or missing. The defenders lost 14 killed and between 19 and 27 wounded. The battle would gain its name from the plantation upon which the fort had been built, the Battle of Red Bank.

The Germans would retreat and eventually retrace their steps to the ships that would ferry

A 1781 painting by William Elliot titled, in part, *Representation of the action off Mud Fort in the River Delaware . . . .* Fort Mifflin was referred to as Mud Fort or Mud Island Fort because "Mud" was the name of the island on which the fortification was located. (nypl)

them back to Philadelphia. Two days later, Washington would send a congratulatory note to Colonel Greene and the defenders on the "happy event and beg you will accept my most particular thanks and present the same to your whole garrison, both officers and men."

The victory would be short-lived, as the entire British effort would turn toward the destruction of Fort Mifflin. It was crucial that the Delaware River be opened for the British garrison to survive the upcoming winter.

Baron Henry Leonard d'Arendt was in charge of Fort Mifflin, but because he was too sick to take command, Lt. Col. Samuel Smith handled the duties of post commander. Smith had the benefit of Maj. Francois-Louis Teissedre de Fleury, another French engineer, serving with him. One of Fleury's improvements was installing a fire step that allowed the defenders to more accurately and resolutely fire over the top of the palisades, and adding a redan to lend support to the main battery. All this was done as the British artillery kept up an incessant bombardment

By November 10, Captain Montresor, using his engineer's training to prepare for the siege, was ready to bring all the weaponry at his disposal to bear on the American fort. In total, the British had two 32-pounders, six 24-pounders, and an 18-pounder. Two 8-inch howitzers, two 8-inch mortars, and a larger 13-inch mortar added additional firepower. With a range of approximately 500 yards, the big guns filled the November day with the sound of shot and the smell of black powder.

Although neither side reported casualties that first day, the following day a spent artillery shell crashed through the barracks in the fort, careened off the brick chimney and struck Lieutenant Colonel Smith in the left hip. Bricks falling from the damaged chimney landed on top of him, and in the process the Pennsylvanian suffered a dislocated wrist. He was evacuated across the river to New Jersey.

The pummeling of Fort Mifflin continued. Major de Fleury wrote to Washington that each night the garrison would come out of hiding to repair the damage done by the British artillery during the preceding daylight hours, but by November 12 all but two artillery pieces had been destroyed. Because of Smith's wounding, Maj. Simeon Thayer assumed command.

Although November 10 was the start of the heavy bombardment, the garrison had been under constant artillery fire since October and conditions continued to deteriorate. Private Joseph Plumb Martin, who spent two grueling weeks as part of the garrison and left an excellent diary of his service in the American Revolution, wrote from inside Fort Mifflin: "We continued here, suffering, cold, hunger, and other miseries...." By November 15, the British Navy had moved "six ships of the line, all sixty-fours, a frigate of thirty six guns, and a gallery" within proximity of the fort. One historian would surmise that with the additions of the night of November 14, "what was probably the largest concentration of firepower of the war was about to be unleashed on Fort Mifflin."

In 1905, an act of the New Jersey Legislature led to the construction of the monument to commemorate the action of Col. Christopher Greene and his Rhode Islanders during the October 22, 1777, defense of Fort Mercer. (es)

The bombardment continued unabated; one shot would claim the lives of five American artillerymen. Major Thayer authorized the garrison to lower the colors on the flagpole, a call for help to the Pennsylvania Navy, which prompted cheering from the British, who thought the fort was going to capitulate. An outcry from the junior officers under Major Thayer prompted the American flag to be raised quickly again, even though it cost a soldier his life when a cannonball struck him. Later that day a cannonball cleaved off a section of the barracks, the debris striking Major Fleury, knocking him unconscious, and disabling another capable and trusted officer of the American garrison.

If that was not enough to endure, Howe had begun preparations to storm the American fort. But on the night of November 14 he postponed the attack to allow the American garrison to evacuate the post after the heavy bombardment that day. He would get his wish.

Major Thayer and the remaining garrison, numbering approximately 300 men, took what they could salvage and under cover of darkness rowed themselves across the Delaware River to New Jersey. A contingent of 40 men lit the barracks on fire around midnight and soon joined their comrades. Leading by example, Major Thayer was the last American to leave Fort Mifflin.

Out of a total garrison of 450 men, the American defenders had suffered approximately 250 casualties from September to the morning of November 16. The British now controlled the Delaware River and on the strength of the British Navy could use the waterway to supply the troops in Philadelphia.

One can still hear a very audible roar when visiting Fort Mifflin today. But instead of British and American artillery, airplanes are the culprits for the sounds. Philadelphia International Airport sits close to Fort Mifflin and jets landing and taking off fly overhead. The site is open Wednesday to Sunday between the hours of 10 a.m. and 4 p.m. from March through mid-December. The website includes the disclaimer that "all other times of the year" they "are open by chance during normal business hours" but instructs potential visitors to call ahead. Check out their website, at fortmifflin. us for updated information.

Fort Mercer is now part of Red Bank Battlefield Park and is open year-round. From mid-April through mid-October, James and Ann Whitall's house, which is historic, is open seasonally for visitation. Special programs are held on certain Sundays throughout the year. For more information and to plan your visit, check out the website for Red Bank Battlefield Park, part of the Gloucester County, New Jersey, web portal.

Detail of Wilmington, 1777. Smallwood's men constructed fortifications at the bridge across the Brandywine at the same locations noted on this map, as well as at the ruins of Fort Christiana (Ancien Fort Apelle Suedois on the map). The Road to Philadelphia and the bridge across the Brandywine corresponds with modern Northeast Boulevard and North Church Street. Taken from *Plan du camp retranchè à Wilmington pour y couvrir notre hospital apres la Battaille de Brandywine* by Friedrich Adam Julius von Wangenheim. (loc)

The Winter Encampment at Wilmington

APPENDIX B
BY TRAVIS SHAW

As the majority of Washington's army settled into winter quarters at Valley Forge, a small detachment was sent nearly 40 miles to the south to establish an outpost at Wilmington, Delaware. Numbering around 1,500 men, they would spend the winter on the banks of Brandywine Creek, guarding the southern approach from British-occupied Philadelphia, interdicting enemy communications and supplies, and suppressing local loyalists. Although they did not share in the hardships at Valley Forge, they faced many of the same difficulties as their comrades, including lack of adequate supplies and harsh weather conditions.

As the 1777 campaign season drew to a close in late November, one of Washington's primary concerns was where to locate his army through the winter. The location needed to have enough forage and shelter for his men, and it needed to be easily defensible. The site also had to be far enough from the British in Philadelphia to remain undisturbed and yet close enough that he could react to any British offensives. Washington considered a number of locations—Lancaster, Bethlehem, Reading, Valley Forge, and Wilmington—and on November 30 he posed the question to a council of his general officers. Each officer weighed the advantages and disadvantages of each site and responded to Washington the following day.

Wilmington, Delaware, held a number of advantages for the Continental army. It lay only 25 miles from Philadelphia, along the west bank of the Delaware River. From this position Washington could threaten British supplies coming by sea. He could also guarantee his own supply lines by keeping the main roads to the southern colonies open and free from British interference. Major General Nathanael Greene wrote in response:

"I cannot help thinking that quarters can be got at Wilmington with much less distress to the Inhabitants of the State—that the position will

Brigadier General William Smallwood, from Maryland, commanded the Continental troops encamped at Wilmington during the winter of 1777-78. (nypl)

be secure enough with the force cantoned in and about it—That provision and forage can be got easier and cheaper in that position than in the other—that from this Position we can draw it from the enemy while the other will leave it for them—that this gives us a better opportunity to protect the lower Jersey, and not less the upper—that this will distress the enemy in drawing supplies—and upon the whole cover a greater extent of country than any other. For these reasons I am for the Position of Wilmington . . . ."

Washington's chief of engineers, Brig. Gen Louis Lebègue Duportail, agreed, stating that by occupying Wilmington the Continental army could deprive the British of valuable resources and recruits and prevent any British evacuation by sea. Another strong voice in favor of taking up winter quarters in Wilmington was Gen. William Smallwood. He echoed his fellow officers, writing that "Wilmington & its vicinage will cover more Troops, & is more compact, may annoy the Enemy, will obstruct them, & cover more of the Country than any Position I am acquainted with under our present Situation. . . ."

Despite the enthusiasm expressed by so many of Washington's subordinates, Wilmington did have several drawbacks. Brigadier General James Irvine argued that Wilmington was too close to Philadelphia, and therefore vulnerable to British attack. Like Irvine, Lafayette also recommended a winter cantonment farther from the enemy, as did Henry Knox, who recommended a position between Lancaster and Reading. Duportail, despite his overall enthusiasm with Wilmington, also cautioned that "it must be confess'd at the same time that these very advantages ought perhaps to prevent our taking it—because the Enemy probably will not suffer us there, and will march out against us."

Washington agreed with this sentiment, but it placed him in a difficult position. Wilmington would make an inviting target if his depleted army were to encamp there, but leaving the town open to British occupation would allow the enemy unfettered access to the Delaware River, the Eastern Shore, and lower New Jersey. Faced with this dilemma, Washington chose to compromise. The bulk of his army would find safety and security at Valley Forge, while a strong detachment would march south and preempt any British attempts to occupy Wilmington. The man chosen to lead this detachment was Brig. Gen. William Smallwood. A native of Charles County, Maryland, Smallwood was a veteran officer of the French and Indian War and a provincial politician. Earlier in the war he had earned renown as the colonel of the Maryland Battalion, which fought a legendary delaying action at the battle of Long Island in August 1776. Although his unit was largely destroyed that summer, Smallwood was soon promoted to brigadier and commanded both Continental troops and Maryland militia during the Philadelphia campaign.

Smallwood was a natural choice for the assignment. Not only had he lobbied for an encampment at Wilmington during Washington's council of war, but he was well acquainted with Delaware and the Eastern Shore of Maryland. During the summer of 1777 he led 500 men across the Chesapeake Bay to suppress growing numbers of loyalists in the region. On December 19 the 45-year-old Marylander received his orders from Washington:

> *Dr Sir,*
> *With the Division lately commanded by Genl Sullivan, you are to March immediately for Wilmington, and take Post there. you are not to delay a moment in putting the place in the best posture of defence, to do which, and for the security of it afterwards, I have written in urgent terms to the President of the Delaware State to give every aid he possibly can of Militia—I have also directed an Engineer to attend you for the purpose of constructing, and superintending*

the Works, and you will fix with the Quarter Master on the number of Tools necessary for the business—but do not let any neglect, or deficiency on his part, impede your operations, as you are hereby vested with full power to sieze & take (passing receipts) such articles as are wanted. The Commissary & Forage Master will receive directions respecting your Supplies, in their way; but I earnestly request that you will see that these Supplies are drawn from the Country between you and Philadelphia, as it will be depriving the Enemy of all chance of getting them; and in this point of view, becomes an object to us of importance.

I earnestly exhort you to keep both Officers and Men to their duty, and to avoid furloughs but in cases of absolute necessity. you will also use your utmost endeavours to collect all the straglers &ca from both Brigades. and you are also to use your best endeavours to get the Men Cloathed in the most comfortable manner you can.

You will be particular in your observation of every thing passing on the River & will communicate every matter of Importance to Dear Sir Yr Most Obedt Sert.

The two brigades assigned to the expedition amounted to approximately 1,500 men, and were comprised of the 1st Delaware Regiment and 1st through 7th Maryland Regiments. Smallwood's command departed the vicinity of Gulph Mills, Pennsylvania, at 4:00 a.m. on December 20 and arrived at Wilmington at 9:00 a.m. the following day after a march of more than 30 miles. As soon as the men arrived they began to fortify the outpost. On December 22 Smallwood reported to Washington that "we have compleated one Battery mounting two Guns at the Bridge; and are now about two more, one on the commanding Ground above that & rather higher up the Brandewine, & another at the Fort late on the Point commanding the two Creeks." Both Smallwood and Washington were keenly aware that the force at Wilmington was not strong enough to repel a determined British attack, and Washington implored the government of Delaware to send all available militia to help augment the force.

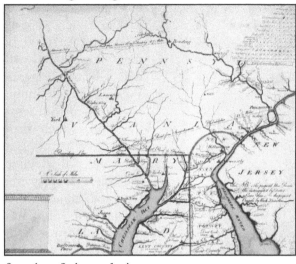

This map of Wilmington and its environs was taken from *Map of proposed roads through the southeastern part of Pennsylvania, the northeastern part of Maryland, and the northern part of Delaware,* published by the American Philosophical Society, 1771. (loc)

Through the end of December the troops settled in along the west bank of the Brandywine, near the intersection of modern Lovering Avenue and Broom Street. Most of their time was spent performing fatigue duties, such as improving their fortifications, foraging for supplies, and observing British shipping in the Delaware River. Smallwood would write to Washington frequently over the coming weeks, relaying valuable information about the movements of supply and troop ships to and from Philadelphia. Smallwood also wrote to complain of the lukewarm response he received from the Delaware militia; by December 27 only 30 men had arrived in his camp to assist his force. The Marylander was also hampered by a lack of horses to patrol the countryside, and his men were desperately lacking shoes.

The monotony of fatigue duty was broken with the capture of local loyalists trying to move in and out of Philadelphia. On December 28, Smallwood relayed that "one of our partys last night intercepted several horse cart loads of provisions by Marcus Hook going to Phila. & took one boatman & 3 country men." The men also busied themselves by intercepting the occasional British vessel. At the end of December a party of Continentals under the command of Captain Erskine took a sloop from the docks at

New Castle loaded with foodstuffs for the British garrison in Philadelphia. As they brought the vessel off it ran aground near Christiana Creek, but after a short run-in with some loyalist sailors Erskine's men were able to secure the ship and its cargo. An even bigger prize was captured the following day when Smallwood got word that a British brig ran aground five miles from Wilmington. He immediately sent a detachment of 100 men with two artillery pieces to capture the ship, which proved to be the transport Symmetry, carrying officers, men, and wives from the 10th Regiment of Foot. The value of the prisoners, however, paled in comparison to the cargo aboard the Symmetry. She carried the baggage of three British Regiments, including tents, uniforms, and stands of arms that the Continental army desperately needed. Lieutenant Colonel Benjamin Ford, writing to Maryland governor Thomas Johnson, referred to the capture as "An excellent New Years Gift for our poor Naked soldiers."

Washington was elated at the news of the Symmetry's capture, but the distribution of the captured equipment strained his relationship with Smallwood. The general officers encamped at Valley Forge demanded that the equipment be brought there to be given to the main army, while the Marylanders maintained that since it was their prize they should keep it. Eventually Washington was able to smooth over the issue, and the Marylanders received much needed uniforms, shoes, and stockings. So many coats were captured that red coats became the standard for Maryland officers that winter and well into 1778.

With the exception of the occasional loyalist or British patrol, the remainder of the winter was quiet for the men in Wilmington. As the men settled back into their routine the biggest challenge faced by Smallwood became desertion. Dozens of men slipped away from the encampment with the hope of either returning home or making their way to the British in Philadelphia. The problem

TRAVIS SHAW *is a native Marylander with a deep love of local history and a full-time contributor to Emerging Revolutionary War.*

was particularly acute among former prisoners or servants given their freedom in exchange for military service. As winter gave way to spring, these losses were largely offset by new recruits arriving from Maryland. Adequate supply also remained a problem, though on a smaller scale than at Valley Forge. A shoe manufacturer was established in an attempt to supply the Wilmington garrison. The Marylanders also did their best to assist the rest of the army, collecting cattle, pork, and flour to forward to Washington's force.

During Smallwood's absence, the army at Valley Forge was reorganized and trained according to the methods of General von Steuben. Not wanting to ignore the brigades at Wilmington, in early May Washington dispatched Lieutenant Colonel Fleury to acquaint them with the new system of drill and maneuver. Washington ordered Smallwood to "choose two active intelligent Officers to do the duty of brigade Inspectors. . . these Gentlemen will receive the Barons written instructions relative to the most elementary points from Col. Fleury, who is perfectly acquainted with his System." The men at Wilmington would not have long to perfect their new drill, however. By mid-May it became clear that the British intended to evacuate Philadelphia, and that Washington would need to concentrate the full force of the army to give chase. On May 17 he wrote to Smallwood, ordering him to prepare to join the main army once the stores at nearby Head of Elk, Maryland, were secured. Nine days later, Smallwood and nearly 1,800 troops began to evacuate Wilmington, followed by a massive wagon train carrying supplies of every sort north to Washington. The winter encampment at Wilmington was over, and Smallwood's Marylanders were on the road that would eventually take them to Monmouth Courthouse.

Determined to Persevere

Of all the places associated with the American War for Independence, perhaps none has come to symbolize perseverance and sacrifice more than Valley Forge. The hardships of the encampment claimed the lives of approximately one in ten, nearly all from disease. Despite the privations suffered by the soldiers at Valley Forge, Washington and his generals built a unified professional military organization that ultimately enabled the Continental Army to triumph over the British.

APPENDIX C
BY PHILLIP S. GREENWALT

As the spring season slowly came to an end in the hills and fields of Pennsylvania, the summer campaigning season would soon beckon the Continental army under Washington back into action against their British and German adversaries. What that ensuing campaign would look like depended on the general officers, but the rank-and-file could look back over a winter encampment of transformation that hardened their resolve.

John Laurens wrote that: "Our men are the best crude materials for soldiers I believe in the world, for they possess a docility and patience which astonish foreigners." One foreigner, the Marquis de Lafayette, echoed similar sentiments and spoke to an underlying reason why history remembers the suffering of the army in general but not the majority of individuals who had been lost. In his "Memoir of 1779," the Frenchman wrote:

[The men] were successively reduced to 5000. . . lacked everything—coats, hats, shirts, and shoes. Their feet and legs turned black with frostbite, and often have to be amputated. For lack of money, they had neither food nor means of transportation. . .[yet] the greatest difficulty in this revolution was always that, in order to hide weakness from the enemy, it was necessary to hide them from the people . . . .

Hide it, deceive the enemy and keep only certain individuals in the Continental Congress informed. The men huddled in their cabins were the recipients of this "deep secret," as Lafayette wrote later in that same publication. That leads us to the question, though, who were the men who had

The mention of Valley Forge is usually synonymous with suffering. The trials, tribulations, and hardships suffered by the thousands of forgotten soldiers overshadow another side of that winter, though—summed up succinctly by the title on this informational panel: a "determination to persevere." What "can't brave Americans endure," truly? (psg) huddled, almost naked, starving, freezing, and wafting between despondency and a sense of hope for change?

Many of their names have been lost in the passage of time, but there are a few facts about these men available today. First, most were single, with a median age between 21 and 25, and a slight majority of them were born in the colonies. For the median age to be in the 20s, there had to be a sizeable portion of the American forces in their teenage years. Studies available today show that teenagers as young as 15 years old, at the onset of the war, joined the militia and what would become the Continental army. In fact, one historian looking at New Jersey enlistment records concluded that nearly 75 percent of boys were 15 or 16 when they joined the cause. Many came from the bottom rungs of society, being laborers, yeoman, or even landless farmers, with many not literate beyond being able to sign their name on enlistment papers.

Historian John Shy depicted the average soldier in the following terms: "As a group, they were poorer, more marginal, less well anchored in society. Perhaps we should not be surprised; it is easy to imagine men like these actually being attracted by the relative affluence, comfort, security, prestige, and even the chance of satisfying human relationships in the Continental Army."

Other historians agree with Shy, writing that Washington's army was comprised of those men "from the disrespected and dispossessed ranks of society" with "little or no property or marketable skill."

Or as Joseph Plumb Martin would write about his reasoning for enlistment: "By and by, they will come swaggering back, thought I, and tell me of their exploits, all their 'hair-breadth 'scapes'. . . O, that was too much to be borne with by me."

Starting the encampment, men suffered from battle wounds still healing and the fatigue of the active campaigning. During the six months at Valley Forge, these ailments would be

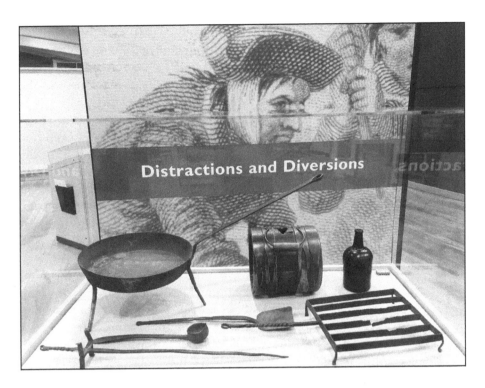

accompanied by various sicknesses, including dysentery, typhoid, typhus, pneumonia, and tuberculosis. Many would suffer from coughs, sniffling noses, colds, and fevers. The poor diet added scurvy and sickness brought on by malnutrition. Add in that, upon arriving in Valley Forge, there were no winter quarters waiting for the men to hunker down in. That type of lodging had to be constructed, and that took time. One account from Capt. William Gifford of New Jersey reported that men under his command had lain "in tents until January 20—an instance of the kind hardly known in any country whatever, but what can't brave Americans endure."

Even night did not bring relief as many of the men lacked blankets, which forced them to sit, kneel, crouch, and hover near the fire to keep warm and to ward off frostbite, then add to that the fact that soap was nonexistent. The daily fortitude of the soldiery stands out even more.

Soldiers throughout the American Revolution became resourceful, reusing or repurposing items to make up for the plethora of shortages they faced. Any distractions from the dreariness and mundane routine of winter were welcomed, as well. (psg)

This depiction of a soldier captured the hardened resolve needed to endure the privations that service in the Continental army entailed. The accompanying ballad conjures up the cold conditions that piled on another element of suffering:

It was a night in winter,
  Some seventy years ago;
The bleak and barren landscape
Was blurred with driving snow.

You caught a glimpse of uplands,
  And guessed where valleys lay;
The trees were broken shadows,
  A house was something gray.

(nypl)

For approximately 3,000 men, the disease, starvation, lack of pay, and destitution that marked the winter was too much to bear and they stole off into the night. Desertion, in their minds, was the best of options.

That number of 3,000 desertions during the six months of the encampment comes from one historian's research. If one extrapolates from the number of officers who resigned, as an example of the incentive to desert from Valley Forge, the plight of the rank-and-file becomes a little more forgiving: "Some fifty Officers at Valley Forge resigned in a single day because their families were not provided for."

The same reasons must have affected the mind and pulled at the heartstrings of the common soldier. Duty to cause was one thing but providing for their families and the chance for a better existence could only come if their families survived. With pay in arrears and foodstuffs being close to non-existent, desertion seemed like a viable option to some, and it's surprising that more did not quit the cause during this winter of transformation.

Why did soldiers stick out the harsh conditions that tormented them that winter? History would have you read that it was for a deep sense of patriotism, but that is only a part of it and more likely post-war reasoning. The chance to obtain land, a source of income, and possibly a fresh start in life for themselves and their families if they had one or had plans to start one following the conflict, were all possible reasons.

Incentives like those mentioned above were attractive to the men. With the promise of land or other non-monetary inducements dependent on a military victory over Great Britain, the soldier had to suffer through the harshness of the winter at Valley Forge as part of the ordeal to have the chance to coup the incentive promised at enlistment.

Congress also cut out the potential to sell these land entitlements when on September 20, 1776, that political body resolved that no officer and/or soldier could sell or otherwise dispose of their land bounty during the war. The rebellious colonies had to win for the soldiers' suffering to be worth something. That kept the men crouched around the campfires during those long winter months.

Another product of sticking with the colors was the benefit of being exposed to soldiers from other states with different ethnic, cultural, and social norms. The word "Continental" was coined in Philadelphia in 1776 by those who hoped to create a harmony among the various colonies and unite them in a single effort to throw off the British yoke. The men in Valley Forge were the living example of that experiment. In a time when the average person rarely left their immediate towns and communities, the chance to see more of the burgeoning country, the thrill and excitement of joining the cause, and afterward being dependent on their military comrades as their de-facto families helped keep the men in Valley Forge.

In terms of different ethnicities, we also know that a percentage of the soldiery at Valley Forge were African-Americans. On February 10, 1778, Rhode Island mustered in three African-American soldiers who were granted their freedom as a reward for their service (their owners were compensated). The prewar free black population of Massachusetts was approximately 4,400 at the outbreak of hostilities. Over 500 of these men would bear arms for the American cause in the Continental army. The colony of Connecticut enlisted nearly 300 African-Americans for the cause of American independence. After looking at records from the beginning of 1778, one historian calculates that 10 percent of the forces at Washington's disposal were African-American. Once again, that number is hard to verify; for example, one company from a mid-Atlantic state listed men with "dark complexions" as African-American but the men in question hailed from Ireland.

Besides African-American and white soldiers native to the 13 colonies, Washington's army also

Even though James Armistead was not present at Valley Forge, Armistead provides an example and portrait of the many African-American faces lost to history that served the patriot cause. Lafayette would later vouch for Armistead's service during the Yorktown campaign. (nypl)

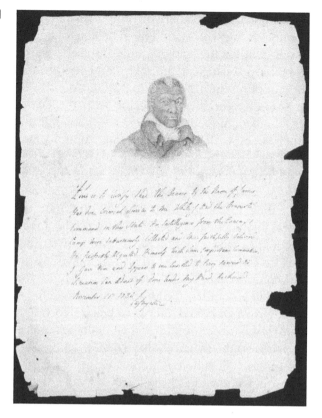

contained soldiers from various European locales. Men from the German states, the Irish, and the Scots-Irish all had native sons bearing arms for the Continental army. As mentioned in previous chapters, the French would formally align their nation with the rebellious colonies, and French officers and men joined the army at Valley Forge as well. Mix in a few Polish sons, and the American army had a sizeable representation of European transplants, adventure seekers, and career soldiers. Other European nations and empires also had subjects sprinkled throughout the ranks.

That is how today one can find as much information about who these nameless faces in paintings, lithographs, and etchings truly were. Though very few accounts from the common soldier have survived the passing of time, the missives that have survived provide enough material for historians to continue to peer into what the world, the suffering, and the transformation that winter at Valley Forge was like for these men. In that regard, their sacrifices and commitment cannot go unrecognized.

Though their names have been lost to the passage of time, enough data exists to piece together the world in which the majority of the common soldiers existed. Sprinkle in the diary accounts that have survived, and we get further insight into their world. However, what is important to history is that these men survived, persevered, and overcame that winter and the long years that followed. Furthermore, the testament to the common soldiers lives on in the victory that they helped ensure. Therefore, we still marvel at what these soldiers, from around the globe and colonies, endured, especially during such a tremendous winter, one that was as transformative as Valley Forge, which helped win the American Revolution.

Even the general in chief recognized the mettle that Valley Forge forged in his soldiers. He would write Congress during that fateful winter: "Naked and starving as they are, we cannot enough admire the incomparable patience and fidelity of the soldiery."

American Gethsemane:
Valley Forge in American Memory

APPENDIX D
BY MARK MALOY

The story of Valley Forge is one of the most heroic and beyond all question the most pathetic chapter in the history of American armies. It required more courage and fortitude to freeze and starve in the cantonments here during the awful winter of 1777 and 1778, than it did to charge the British Regulars in the open field, or to assault them in the redoubts at Yorktown.
– Congressman Champ Clark, Dedication of the Memorial Arch, 1917

Valley Forge holds a treasured place in the memory of the American people. No other winter encampment of the American Revolutionary War is remembered quite like Valley Forge. Cambridge, Morristown, Middlebrook, New Windsor, Newburgh; none conjure up as much emotion or imagery, despite the importance each of those encampments played in the ultimate success of the Revolutionary War. The very words 'Valley Forge' immediately bring to mind terrifying images of battered soldiers with no shoes or food hunkered around a fire on a dreary, snowy evening. The sacrifice and perseverance of those soldiers instantly instills a sense of pride and patriotism that few other events do. In fact, no other military encampment in any war is remembered in quite the same way as Valley Forge. Even the more popularly remembered American Civil War has no equivalent. One British historian, Sir George Otto Trevelyan, declared Valley Forge to be "the most celebrated encampment in the world's history."

Despite its status in history and memory, much of what we learn about Valley Forge in grade school is not entirely accurate. The very first thing most people picture when they hear 'Valley Forge' is a frozen tundra covered in snow and ice. However, as described earlier in this book, the winter of 1777–78 was

The image of Washington praying at Valley Forge became so ubiquitous in the early 20th century that a bas relief was placed at Federal Hall in New York City where Washington was inaugurated president in 1789. (wc)

a fairly typical one with no major blizzard-like snows, and the temperature dropped into single digits only a couple of times. Compare that with the Morristown winter encampment two years later in 1779–80. During that winter, the absolute worst of the 18th century, New Jersey had 26 snowstorms, and six of those were blizzards.

Every saltwater inlet from North Carolina to Canada froze over completely. In fact, in New York harbor the ice was so thick that British soldiers were able to march from Manhattan to Staten Island on it. Some snowfalls measured more than four feet with drifts over six feet. The temperature only made it above freezing a couple of times in the whole winter. Even General Washington noted after the winter of 1779–1780 that "the oldest people now living in this Country do not remember so hard a winter as the one we are now emerging from. In a word the severity of the frost exceeded anything of the kind that had ever been experienced in this climate before." Even though the winter at Valley Forge was not as cold or snowy, the warmer weather turned much of the encampment into a muddy quagmire. This made it difficult for the soldiers to drill or work and also brought about very unsanitary conditions in the camp that resulted in an increase in the amount of disease and death. Though the image of large snow drifts in the Valley Forge encampment did not occur that winter, it did not lessen the suffering and sacrifice of the men.

The story of Washington's prayer at Valley Forge reinforced many Americans' belief that the cause of American independence had been divinely ordained by God. (loc)

In addition to the sight of soldiers freezing in the snow, the image of the commanding general, George Washington, hatless, kneeling next to his horse in a snowy glen, praying to God for the deliverance of his army has been one of the most popular and powerful images of the founding of the United States. President Ronald Reagan called it the "most sublime image in American history." The image first became popular in the early 19th century, and that popularity has continued into the present day. The scene has inspired numerous paintings, etchings, drawings, postage stamps, and statues.

This story originated with Mason Locke Weems, better known as Parson Weems, the same man who created the story about Washington chopping down a cherry tree down as a child. The story was originally published in 1800 in Weems's book, The Life of Washington. In his

A. Gilbert drew and painted this sketch in 1843 of General Washington and Lafayette visiting the "suffering part of the army" during the Valley Forge encampment. (nypl)

retelling, a local Quaker, Isaac Potts, was walking through the snowy woods near Valley Forge and came upon "the commander in chief of the American armies on his knees at prayer!" Potts ran home to his wife and told her that he thought "the sword and the gospel were utterly inconsistent," but that seeing Washington praying had changed his mind.

Did this actually happen? There are no contemporary accounts of anyone having seen Washington pray openly at Valley Forge, and the Weems story was likely created by him as a parable meant to highlight Washington's Christian virtue. Weems had been known to fabricate stories like the cherry story to embellish this trait in Washington. The unfortunate part of this, though, is that Washington's virtues needed no embellishment. Throughout the 19th and 20th centuries, almost every religious group wanted to claim Washington as one of their own. There is even an outlandish tale that Washington converted to Catholicism on his deathbed. The prayer at Valley Forge story was used by many Christians to demonstrate his personal religious

The United States Army remembered with pride the devotion of the soldiers at Valley Forge. (na)

beliefs and God Almighty's official blessing on the cause of American independence.

Today, George Washington's actual religious beliefs and practices are a matter of intense historical debate. While he did attend church services and many times expressed his belief in Divine Providence, Washington also did not take communion and rarely referred to Jesus Christ.

While his personal beliefs have caused much debate over the past 250 years, most historians agree that the Parson Weems story was just that, a story. However, while most historians would agree that Washington would not have prayed in the open as Weems described, it could very well have been the case that he did so privately in his headquarters. Regardless, the scene still remains an incredibly powerful image. Ronald Reagan said, "That image personifies a people who know that it's not enough to depend on our own courage and goodness. We must also seek help from God our father and preserver." While we often think of the Founding Fathers, and especially George Washington, as cool, calm, and in control of the destiny of the nation, at places like Valley Forge that was very much not the case. The image of Washington praying in the woods reinforces that very real fact.

Some of the imagery of the Valley Forge encampment, though, we know actually did happen. The frequent stories of men suffering frostbite and marching in the wintry conditions with no shoes, leaving bloody footprints in the snow are true. Washington and his officers wrote often of the supply problems and common lack of footwear for the soldiers. And while Valley Forge was not the only instance of this in the war, it did happen. To think of the pain such injuries would cause and the mettle of the men who endured it is difficult to comprehend.

Why was it that Valley Forge has been remembered and not the other encampments? Unlike all the others, not only was Valley Forge a terrible ordeal endured by the American soldiers, it also made for a great story that had some important redemptive qualities. The winter took place at a crucial point in the Revolutionary War. After having lost the American capital, Philadelphia, the Continental Army became the representative of the Patriot cause, and Washington needed to keep the army together for the cause to continue to live. He was successful in that, and with the aid of Baron von Steuben was able to create a stronger and more professional army over the course of the winter. At Valley Forge, the Continental Army suffered and bled but came back the following summer more powerful than when it had entered. When the army marched out of Valley Forge in June of 1778, they were able to fight the professional British Army at Monmouth Court House to a draw. Valley Forge became to Americans what historian Joseph Ellis described as "a place enshrined in mythology ever since as a kind of American Gethsemane, where Washington, the American Christ, kneels in prayer amidst bloodstained snow beseeching the Lord for deliverance."

The soldiers were also extremely patient in their suffering at Valley Forge. Despite the horrid conditions and the lack of faith in the cause, the core of Washington's army withstood these horrors and survived.

Copyright, New York Evening Post Co.   CESARE in New York Evening Post
TWO WINTERS
Washington, 1917   Valley Forge, 1777

The image of Washington at Valley Forge has been used throughout the years as a symbol of perseverance in the face of adversity, such as in the uncertain times of World War I. (loc)

Unlike the winter at Morristown, there was no large mutiny during the Valley Forge encampment. While there was discontent among the soldiers, they never organized in defiance. At Valley Forge Washington not only kept his army together, he also succeeded in quashing a cabal. And it was here that he learned of the French joining the military effort on the American side. For all these reasons and more, Valley Forge was a turning point in the war, and that deserved remembering.

While numerous stories and myths were created or embellished about this Continental Army encampment, what inspired these fabrications was a truly tragic and noble event. It is still important to remember that 12,000 men marched into Valley Forge in December of 1777, and almost 2,500 of them died of disease, malnutrition and exposure. That is a death rate of around 20 percent. More men died here than at any other winter encampment of the war (and more than any battle of the war) and that is probably a major reason it has been seared into American memory. The sacrifice laid upon the altar of liberty at Valley Forge was astounding.

Valley Forge still matters to us today. The scene of the horrid encampment is now preserved as a beautiful park interpreted by the National Park Service. Hundreds of thousands of Americans make the pilgrimage to Valley Forge every year to learn about what did and what did not happen there. While not all the stories told about Valley Forge are true, the sacrifice, perseverance, and devotion to duty exhibited by Washington and his army that winter are still remembered. This is as it should be. It was the winter that won the war.

MARK MALOY *is a historian currently working for the National Park Service in Virginia. He is the author of* Victory or Death: The Battles of Trenton and Princeton, December 25, 1776 – January 3, 1777, *one of the inaugural volumes in the Emerging Revolutionary War Series.*

WINTER ENCAMPMENT

Commanding Gen.: Gen. George Washington
Staff: Lt. Col. Alexander Hamilton, Lt. Col. John Laurens,
Lt. Col. Robert Harrison, Lt. Col. Richard Meade, Lt. Col. Tench Tilghman
Life Guards: Capt. Caleb Gibbs

Military Staff
Staff Officer: Maj. Gen. John Sullivan
Quartermaster: Maj. Gen. Thomas Mifflin, Maj. Gen. Nathanael Greene
Inspector General: Maj. Gen. Thomas Conway, Brig. Gen. Baron Frederich
von Steuben
Engineer: Col. Louis DuPortail

FIRST DIVISION: Maj. Gen. Charles Lee
Varnum's Brigade: Brig. Gen. James Varnum
4th Connecticut · 8th Connecticut · 1st Rhode Island · 2nd Rhode Island

Poor's Brigade: Brig. Gen. Enoch Poor
1st New Hampshire · 2nd New Hampshire · 3rd New Hampshire
2nd New York · 4th New York

Huntington's Brigade: Brig. Gen. Jedediah Huntington
1st Connecticut · 2nd Connecticut · 5th Connecticut · 7th Connecticut

SECOND DIVISION: Maj. Gen. Thomas Mifflin, Brig. Gen. Anthony Wayne (Acting)
Wayne's Brigade: Brig. Gen. Anthony Wayne
1st Pennsylvania · 2nd Pennsylvania · 7th Pennsylvania · 10th Pennsylvania
Hartley's Regiment

2nd Pennsylvania Brigade:
4th Pennsylvania · 5th Pennsylvania · 8th Pennsylvania · 11th Pennsylvania
1st New York

Late Conway's Brigade:
3rd Pennsylvania · 6th Pennsylvania · 9th Pennsylvania · 12th Pennsylvania
Malcolm's Addition · Spencer's Addition

Third DIVISION: Maj. Gen. Marquis de Lafayette
North Carolina Brigade: Brig. Gen. Lachlan McIntosh
1st North Carolina · 2nd North Carolina · 3rd North Carolina
4th North Carolina · 5th North Carolina · 6th North Carolina · 7th North Carolina
8th North Carolina · 9th North Carolina · 10th North Carolina

4th Virginia Brigade: Brig. Gen. Charles Scott
4th Virginia · 8th Virginia · 12th Virginia · Patton's Regiment
Grayson's Regiment

3rd Virginia Brigade: Brig. Gen. William Woodford
3rd Virginia · 7th Virginia · 11th Virginia · 15th Virginia

FOURTH DIVISION: Maj. Gen. Baron Johann de Kalb
3rd Massachusetts Brigade: Brig. Gen. John Patterson
10th Massachusetts · 11th Massachusetts · 12th Massachusetts · 14th Massachusetts

4th Massachusetts Brigade: Brig. Gen. Ebenezer Learned
2nd Massachusetts · 8th Massachusetts · 9th Massachusetts

2nd Massachusetts Brigade: Brig. Gen. John Glover
1st Massachusetts · 4th Massachusetts · 13th Massachusetts · 15th Massachusetts

FIFTH DIVISION: Maj. Gen. William Alexander, Lord Stirling
1st Virginia Brigade: Brig. Gen. Peter Muhlenberg
1st Virginia · 5th Virginia · 9th Virginia · 13th Virginia · 1st Virginia State
2nd Virginia State · German Regiment

2nd Virginia Brigade: Brig. Gen. George Weedon
2nd Virginia · 6th Virginia · 10th Virginia · 14th Virginia · 13th Pennsylvania

*1st Maryland Brigade: Brig. Gen. William Smallwood
1st Delaware · 1st Maryland · 3rd Maryland · 5th Maryland · 7th Maryland

*2nd Maryland Brigade:
2nd Maryland · 4th Maryland · 6th Maryland

UNATTACHED (SUPPORT)
New Jersey Brigade: Brig. Gen. William Maxwell
1st New Jersey · 2nd New Jersey · 3rd New Jersey · 4th New Jersey

Artillery: Brig. Gen. Henry Knox
1st Artillery · 2nd Artillery · 3rd Artillery · 4th Artillery

Cavalry: Brig. Gen. Casimir Pulaski, Col. Stephan Moylan (Acting)
1st Dragoons · 2nd Dragoons · 3rd Dragoons · 4th Dragoons

*The 1st and 2nd Maryland Brigades were encamped at Wilmington, Delaware through most of the winter, returning to the main army in May

Suggested Reading
VALLEY FORGE

The Philadelphia Campaign: Brandywine and the Fall of Philadelphia, Volume I
Thomas J. McGuire
Stackpole Military History Series (2006)
ISBN: 0811701786

McGuire, the preeminent historian of this campaign, uses in-depth research to uncover a plethora of primary sources to construct the first of the two volumes of his study on the Philadelphia campaign. The volumes give a complete look at this 1777 campaign.

The Philadelphia Campaign: Germantown and the Roads to Valley Forge, Volume II
Thomas J. McGuire
Stackpole Military History Series (2007)
ISBN: 0811702065

The second volume of the exhaustive study of the campaign.

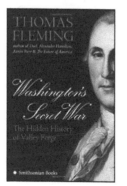

Washington's Secret War: The Hidden History of Valley Forge
Thomas Fleming
HarperCollins Publishing (2005)
ISBN: 0060829621

A detailed study of Valley Forge and the various issues that surrounded George Washington and his men during this pivotal winter of the American Revolution.

*The Drillmaster of Valley Forge: The Baron de Steuben
and the Making of the American Army*
Paul Lockhart
HarperCollins Publishing (2010)
ISBN: 0061451649

A great overview of the life of Baron Frederich von Steuben and his importance to the Continental army during the winter of Valley Forge.

Brandywine: A Military History of the Battle that Lost Philadelphia but Saved America, September 11, 1777.
Michael C. Harris
Savas Beatie (2017)
ISBN: 1611213223

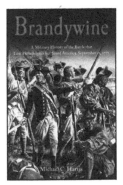

The largest battle, in terms of manpower and acreage of the field of combat, fought in the entire American Revolution, the book provides an overview of the battle plus the campaign that surrounds this engagement on September 11, 1777.

Valley Forge: A Genesis for Command and Control, Continental Army Style
Herman O. Benninghoff, II
Thomas Publications (2001)
ISBN: 1577470656

In this groundbreaking study, Benninghoff uses the aspects of command and control, modern military terminology, and transfixes them to study the Continental army during the winter of Valley Forge.

The Heart of Everything That is Valley Forge
Bob Drury & Tom Clavin
Simon & Shuster (2018)
ISBN: 9781501152719

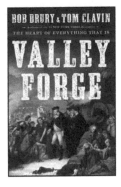

An overview and general history of the encampment at Valley Forge and the transformation that occurred during those months in Pennsylvania.

About the Author

Phillip S. Greenwalt is the co-founder of the Emerging Revolutionary War blog and a full-time contributor to Emerging Civil War. Phill graduated from George Mason University with a M.A. in American History and also has a B.A. in history from Wheeling Jesuit University. He is currently a Supervisory Park Ranger in Interpretation and Visitor Services for Everglades National Park.

EMERGING REVOLUTIONARY WAR SERIES